STILL
ALIVE

STILL ALIVE

A Wild Life of Rediscovery

BY FORREST GALANTE

The World's Leading Rare Species Expert and Host of *Extinct or Alive*

hachette
BOOKS
NEW YORK

Hachette Books

Hachette Book Group

1290 Avenue of the Americas

New York, NY 10104

HachetteBooks.com

Twitter.com/HachetteBooks

Instagram.com/HachetteBooks

First Edition: June 2021

Published by Hachette Books, an imprint of Perseus Books, LLC, a subsidiary of Hachette Book Group, Inc. The Hachette Books name and logo is a trademark of the Hachette Book Group.

The Hachette Speakers Bureau provides a wide range of authors for speaking events. To find out more, go to www.hachettespeakersbureau.com or call (866) 376-6591.

The publisher is not responsible for websites (or their content) that are not owned by the publisher.

Print book interior design by Linda Mark.

Library of Congress Cataloging-in-Publication Data

Names: Galante, Forrest, author.

Title: Still alive : a wild life of rediscovery / by Forrest Galante, host of Extinct or Alive and the world's no. 1 rare species expert.

Description: First edition. | New York : Hachette Books, 2021.

Identifiers: LCCN 2021002220 | ISBN 9780306924279 (hardcover) | ISBN 9780306924262 (ebook)

Subjects: LCSH: Galante, Forrest. | Adventure and adventurers—United States—Biography. | Rare animals—Conservation. | Rare animals—Habitat—Conservation.

Classification: LCC QL82 .G35 2021 | DDC 591.68092 [B]—dc23

LC record available at https://lccn.loc.gov/2021002220

ISBNs: 978-0-306-92427-9 (hardcover); 978-0-306-92426-2 (ebook)

Printed in the United States of America

LSC-C

Printing 1, 2021

To my mother, Jacaranda,
for always supporting my passion for animals
and never telling me to "get a real job."

I just wish the world was twice as big
and half of it was still unexplored.

—SIR DAVID ATTENBOROUGH

CONTENTS

Contents

PREFACE

I t was hot. Early summer. The temperature had been in the mid-nineties all day as I caught as many Southern Pacific rattlesnakes as I could. I was barely twenty years old and working as a biological field tech for the University of California, Santa Barbara, and my job was to handle large, venomous pit vipers. I would catch them, put some paint around their tails, and insert a radio transmitter so we could find them later. I could not have imagined a better job. I was out on my own in a beautiful place, catching rattlesnakes and working as a real biologist.

On one such day, running around the Chimineas Preserve, a transitional landscape where the rolling grasslands of Southern California meet the granite outcroppings of the western Sierras with scrub oaks dispersed between them, I was looking for my final snake of the day. I had banded eleven so far. Most of the other techs had already knocked off with three or four. But I was relentless. I was motivated. I wanted my even dozen. As you will come to see, I am never one to head home early. I was looking in every crack and crevice, beneath every log and shrub, but I wasn't finding anything. It was getting late in the day, so I decided to climb up a rocky outcropping jutting up from the ground. I figured I would get to the top, look around for the car, and see if I had to make my way home before dark. I started climbing up this crumbly cliff. I probably could have gone the long way around. I probably could have just guessed the direction of where my car was parked, but, again, I was twenty. Why wouldn't I scramble up this rock face? It was about twenty feet high and full of cracks, fissures, and all sorts of hidey-holes. I was about halfway up the cliff when I came to a ledge jutting out slightly above me. I reached up with my left hand and took hold. I reached up with my right and did the same. I pulled myself up slowly, searching with my feet until I found a firm place to plant my boot, and as my hairline, then eyebrows, and then eyeballs crested the ledge, I beheld a perfectly coiled Southern Pacific rattlesnake centered between my two hands. As I said, it was hot. The snakes were fired up. My hands had agitated this venomous viper, and even before I came eye level to it, the snake was in motion. All I saw was the inside of a rattlesnake's mouth, a fresh pink gullet with four needle-like fangs flying toward my face. The top two fangs pointed at my eyebrows and the bottom two brushed against my eyelashes. And in an instinctive effort to escape, I pushed off the ledge with all of my strength and flew backward into space.

I should probably introduce myself. My name is Forrest Galante. I am a wildlife biologist and, on my show, *Extinct or Alive*, I bring species back from the dead. But my work doesn't take place in a lab. Instead, I venture into some of the most remote and wildest places left on Earth to find animals that humanity has given up for extinct. This book is my story so far, my chance to share how I grew from a barefoot boy in the Zimbabwean bush, to a young biologist working along the coast of California, to a pioneering adventurer with a grand mission and a host of unprecedented discoveries.

But back to the snake. I fell about eight or nine feet straight onto my back, knocking the wind completely out of me. I rolled over and heaved myself up onto all fours, taking big, noisy, desperate gulps of air. As soon as I recovered, I started touching my face (this was before cell phones with selfie cameras), searching for where the snake had caught me. I kept thinking my eyes were swelling shut, that my vision was blurring, but it was all a panicked reaction. I was, by some miracle of timing and physics, perfectly fine.

And now I knew where the twelfth snake was.

INTRODUCTION

INTRODUCTION

I wasn't a bad kid, but I was wild.

I grew up on a 200-acre farm in Zimbabwe on the outskirts of the capital, Harare. Our land was set upon ironstone soil, red dirt African bush, a landscape abounding with granite outcroppings and Miombo woodland. I lived there with my mother, sister, and 200 workers, along with their families. We grew oranges, avocadoes, and flowers. It was an idyllic place, and mine was an idyllic childhood.

I spent what seemed like the majority of my boyhood, when not in school or in the deep bush, by the dam on our farm, stalking the banks of "the big lake." My friends were the children of the farmworkers. We spoke to one another in English and Shona as we honed our skills catching snakes, fish, and turtles. At seven or eight years old, outfitted with a hook, a worm, and a piece of line tied to a bamboo pole, we caught two-inch-long bream, flinging them one after the other onto the bank, where we built small fires and cooked them right there. For seasoning, we used the salt we had shoved in our pockets before leaving the house. We never packed a lunch or took water. We ate what we caught and drank from the dam's outlet. We constructed bows and arrows and shot targets. We built rafts to brave the waters of the lake, which always felt like an adventure. Some nights I slept on the floor of a worker's *rondavel*, which is an African mud house with a thatched roof. Other nights my friends joined me in our house. It was a happy if tenuous place.

My home was full of animals. Above my bed, sleeping in the mosquito netting, was our vervet monkey, Chippy. We found him in a field we were plowing, abandoned by his troop for what we later learned was a heart murmur, and he became my best friend. When I woke up in the morning, he would jump down onto my shoulders, accompanying me to break-fast. When I left for school, he'd take to the trees, descending only when I returned at the end of the day.

Gliding through the house were my mother's two servals, large, elegant, wild cats, native to Zimbabwe, that we had res-cued as kittens. They enjoyed beating up on our Rhodesian ridgebacks, and visitors to our house were genuinely terrified of them. It is a good thing their tenure didn't overlap with the blue duiker's, a small, forest antelope that trotted our halls for a time.

My room was a lively place. Some kids have video games; some have rock 'n' roll posters. I had wall-to-wall terrariums, fourteen in total, one-half of which housed snakes, and the other half contained my collection of freshwater fish, each tank representing a different region in Zimbabwe and a different type of body of water. It wasn't enough to live in a wild and beautiful country; I had to share my every waking and non-waking moment with animals. My love for them began before I can even remember.

This book, this story I have to tell about my journey so far and the amazing animals that inspire me, is about how that inborn passion survived for so long, despite what life would throw at my family and me, and how my happy obsession with the creatures of this world has guided me through the threshold of discovery time and again. I want to show how a love of nature can shape a life and change the world.

I invite you to travel with me to the wildest places left on Earth to find animals that humanity has given up for extinct, while I share stories of adventure and discovery, of finding your tribe and fighting for your beliefs, and of animals lost and found.

1

LIFE IN ZIMBABWE

LIFE IN ZIMBABWE

remember the moment clearly: the stabbing pain, my skin peeling against the restrictive leather, and my toes packed against one another within my miniature oxfords. I was six years old, and this was the first time I had ever really worn a pair of shoes. I hated them straightaway and asked my mother if I could take them off. I couldn't believe it when she said I had to wear them all day at school. My discomfort with those shoes was only the beginning of my discomfort with formal education. I've always learned better in the wild.

At age thirteen, I entered Form One at St. John's College. It was all brick, all boys, and all very strict rules, an antiquated school system left over from the days of colonial government. Students walked in straight lines and always said, "Good morning, sir. Good morning, ma'am." Everyone in the school had to have the same haircut, uniform, and tie. I had my head shaved in front of the whole school because my hair was touching my ears. We sang war cries, which were like the pre-match *haka* chants of New Zealand's All Blacks rugby team, except we were hundreds of schoolboys packed into a gymnasium, dressed in green and gray. Our school pride was fierce and total, and we took tradition seriously.

I was known as a "squack," which meant I was the personal servant of a prefect, charged with greeting him every morning, carrying his books, making his tea, and otherwise making myself available to meet his every whim. If I failed to uphold the requirements of this relationship or, worse, if I out and out defied them, the punishment was severe. Once, in retaliation for I don't know what, I spat on the prefect's lawn. He gave me a caning so bad I couldn't sit down for a week.

Although I managed to keep up my grades, I did not do well under the heavy structure. I did not enjoy being told what to do. Who does? And so, I would watch the clock and count the hours until school was over. The moment we were released, I would kick off my shoes, loosen the tie around my neck, unbutton my shirt, and run for my ride back to the farm. Once there, I'd sprint toward the compound where all my friends lived, gather them up, and then run down to the dam to fish and catch animals. Every now and again we'd break from routine, like the time we built a jackal pit, intending to trap a jackal, but trapping an unsuspecting farm kid instead. We were so nervous about getting in trouble that we never told anyone, and he was stuck in the hole for hours. I blame Robinson Crusoe for that bright idea.

Life in Zimbabwe

Kicking around the lake and chasing animals is good fun for any kid, but even at a young age, I knew I owed nature something in return for all I so enjoyed. I recall the morning before school when my sister playfully, or maybe not so playfully, threw a pair of pruning clippers at me. She meant to stop me from teasing her, which she did, in addition to filleting my calf open. My mother took one look at the wound and said, "You need to go to the hospital." Normally, on the farm we would stitch ourselves up, but we had just recently run out of antiseptic. As we prepared to leave, the groom, Fani, came running up and said, "Madam, madam! One of the cows is dying." It turned out that, in the field, Daisy the Friesian cow was trying to give birth, but the calf was stuck in the birth canal, and both mother and calf looked to be moments away from expiring.

I had torn my T-shirt into strips to bandage my gash and slow the bleeding. I was sitting there, nine years old, wondering, do we stay or do we go? My mother then left the decision to me: "Forrest, you have a decision to make. We can either go to the hospital and get your leg fixed right now, or we can wait and try to save this cow and save the calf."

Of course, I decided to stay, to save the cow. It took hours, but we helped a beautiful, little, patchy black-and-white calf into the world. Its mother, unfortunately, died after the lengthy birth, and the little calf lived in our garage, where I bottle-fed him every day until he was big enough to join the herd. We named him Stitch, after the stitches I had foregone to save it. I remember thinking then that it was much more important to protect life than to worry about my own temporary pain. I still have the scar as a reminder.

◇ ◇ ◇

MY FATHER LEFT US WHEN I WAS SEVEN YEARS OLD, LEAVING THE responsibility of raising two children while earning a living to my mother. Her farm was one source of income, but her ability to manage the farm was complicated by Shona culture, wherein men do not take orders from women. In their culture, women are commodities to be traded as wives in exchange for livestock. But when a boy turns ten or eleven years old, he is considered a man. So, I became my mother's mouthpiece, delivering her instructions and essentially helping to run a farm of 200 workers. I would receive the days' orders from my mother and then stand, dressed in my school uniform, on a crate or stump to direct different groups of workers to one field or another. The instructions may have been my mother's, but I was expected to see them through, supervising from one phase of a job to the next. I often didn't understand what I was doing, but, in Africa, you find a way to survive.

My mother's other source of income, and something that brought immense joy into my life, was her work as a professional hunter/guide (PH). To be clear, a PH is the term for a safari guide in Zimbabwe. My mother was not stalking animals to kill. Like me, she was a conservationist. She spent years studying to become a PH as well as to earn her pilot's license. She was one of the first female bush pilots in southern Africa and one of the first female safari guides. School in Zimbabwe is three months on and one month off, so every break we'd take off for the bush, usually either to the Limpopo Valley on the border with South Africa or Mana Pools on the border with Zambia, the latter being my favorite place on Earth.

There is no place else on the planet where you are more a part of the food chain or where you see what Africa should be like. Mana Pools is full of megafauna. At every turn, there are elephants, cape buffalo, wildebeest, zebra, and impala. At night, the air comes alive with the sound of lions roaring across the valley. There are leopards. There are hyenas. The food chain is perfectly intact. Because Mana Pools has been a national park for so long, the animals are not negatively conditioned against people, unlike everywhere else where they have been hunted. We'd go on foot through the bush—Mana Pools is one of the last places in Africa where you can still go on a walking safari—and the animals wouldn't dart away or flee out of fear. They just go about their business. It is a wild land of fierce innocence. Not only that, but it is stunning. The savanna teems with animals small and large, living together on the banks of the Zambezi River, which, for my money, is the most remarkable piece of water on Earth. The river sweeps over the landscape, brimming with huge, toothy tiger fish. Massive crocodiles are so abundant that they can line both sides of the river from head to tail. Pods of hippos call to one another, filling the air, alongside the calls of lilac-breasted rollers and guinea fowl, with the busy noise of life. They say creatures and civilizations alike crawled out of Africa. But I think they all crawled from the Zambezi Valley. It is a place out of time, an Edenic jewel, a prism through which we can see what the whole world should look like. If I could live there, I would. But a month at a time had to do.

During our month in the bush, I would be stuck at camp a lot of the time, washing dishes, setting up tents, and the like. If my mom wasn't busy, she would teach me how to shoot, how to track. When she guided clients, she led them on walking safaris, which is not what most honeymooners sign up for these days. She wasn't driving a Land Rover in circles like a tour at Disneyland. She was flying her clients in her Cessna aircraft to a dirt landing strip, meeting a safari vehicle that drove them to camp, and then leading them to wildlife on foot. And when she was afield with clients, I would sneak off whenever I could, flipping logs and catching cobras, tracking lions when nobody was looking, baiting hyenas, and doing all kinds of naughty things that are likely to get little boys killed. Without a shadow of a doubt, those are my happiest memories.

Once, back when my mother was still training for her PH, we traveled to the bush with my mother's parents. I was obsessed with fishing (still am) and wanted to catch a tigerfish in the Zambezi River. Tigerfish are voracious predators with a mouthful of overlarge teeth. My grandpa gamely volunteered to take me. He was a good bushman—no PH or accreditation, just someone with a sure sense of how to conduct himself in the wild. We walked down to the Zambezi River in Mana Pools National Park and began casting spinners into eddies swirling off the main current. The action was slow until we were soon joined by some unexpected company: a giant bull elephant coming down the same gully we had taken to the riverbank, cutting us off from camp.

As the elephant approached our position, my mother called out to warn us, keeping her voice steady and calm, knowing that any signal of panic would immediately translate to the animal. My grandfather said to me, "Don't move. If you run, you will die." And this big, wild bull elephant, an animal not used to people, continued down to the water for a drink and looked over at us. We were both dead still. We were watching for the worst, unsure of what we would do if the "elly" decided to charge. "Don't do anything," my grandfather repeated. And we didn't. Or I didn't do anything except for what I was already doing, which was fishing. I cast my lure back into the water, probably about three feet from the gray monolith's trunk. My grandfather chuckled as we all continued to calmly go about our business. We were only fifteen or twenty feet away from the elephant and somehow, slowly, the danger of the moment evaporated so that we could sit there and enjoy the spectacle of this creature. He seemed to have decided that we weren't posing a threat and so languidly drank his fill. Afterward, my grandfather commended me for being so brave because if I had run, the elephant would have come over and trampled me. That is what animals do in the bush. But I held my ground, not threatening the animal and not cowering, either.

People like to joke about Australia being dangerous. Those people have obviously never been to Africa. Australia has a few snakes and a lot of kangaroos, whereas African fauna, at every level of the food chain, has the size, speed, and ferocity to trample or eat you at will. Still, while Africa is exceptional in many ways, there is a generic truism that applies even here: you can count on an animal to act in its own interest. Its behavior expresses the rationality of survival. But only the actions of your fellow man can truly surprise you.

◇ ◇ ◇

AFRICA ISN'T A GENTLE PLACE, AND OUR FARM WAS NO EXCEP-tion. The workers would drink scud—lumpy, disgusting, corn-fermented beer brewed by the locals—every Saturday night. And every Saturday night bad things would happen.

For my tenth birthday, I received a PeeWee 50 Yamaha dirt bike. This sweet machine, called a *mdudu* bike in Shona, was my new ride to the dam, when previously I would ride a horse or just run. One weekend, not long after I graduated to this new mode of transportation, I was riding the PeeWee on a dirt track off the main road, through one of the grass fields. I saw in the distance a branch of one of the big mahogany trees hanging strangely, as if being weighed down. I noticed because I was always looking in trees for snakes, birds, or Chippy. I rode my bike toward the strange branch, all alone on a little foot trail, as the shape began to materialize into some-one I recognized. "Oh, there's Wireless," I thought. He was the carpenter, whose job it was to cut all the wood for small projects around the farm. As I got closer, I realized Wireless was hanging by his neck on a piece of wire. I was confused.

I stared up at him. At ten years old, I couldn't quite conceive of someone being dead, but I remember a sinking feeling of wrongness. I shouted up to him, "Wireless, wake up! Wireless, wake up!" But he didn't. I grabbed his leg and shook him. He didn't move. I got back on my mdudu bike and went to find my mother. Wireless never woke up. Everyone on the farm said he killed himself. No one paid much attention to the fact that Wireless's shoes and wallet were missing.

Zimbabwe was a trying place at the best of times, even when food was abundant, and things like what happened to Wireless were a regular occurrence. I remember hearing stories about farmers turning up murdered, even years before the chaos of land reformation. These crimes were isolated, unsolved events. Understandably, we were wary when two slick-looking city guys arrived at our farm, hoping to buy $10,000 worth of oranges. This was a highly unusual request. On average, we sold bags of oranges for five or ten dollars. But my mother said she would be happy to sell them that amount and asked how they would be paying. They provided a check in the name of a Mr. A. Johnson. A simple look at the buyers could tell you that neither one of them was a Mr. Johnson. They were more likely a Mr. Tendai or a Mr. Mapfumo. My mother went to her office to determine the whereabouts of Mr. Johnson and quickly learned that he had been murdered the day before. These two thugs had been going from one farm to the next, stealing what they could and then using their gains to barter or worse at the next farm. My mother called the police. This being Zimbabwe, the police assured her they would be there in one or two hours, so we had time to kill with two dangerous guests on our doorstep. With a revolver now tucked into the back of her waistband, my mother reemerged to assure the gentlemen that we were getting their oranges ready.

At some point during the wait, one of the buyers decided to expedite the process by pulling out a sizeable *panga*, which is like a curved machete, and lunged to slash my mother. Before he could, my mother shot him in the thigh with her revolver. His associate, thinking better of the deal, made to run; but our security guard, along with my mother, persuaded him to stay until the police arrived. We restrained the pair with ropes to a fig tree in our front garden.

I had been watching the action from my bedroom window, where I had spears and bows and arrows hanging on my wall, collected by my mother from all over the continent, as far as northern Kenya to the tip of southern Africa. So, thinking that I would help the cause of defending our home, I ran out of the house and shot an arrow into the other thigh of the already wounded would-be killer. The terrible scolding I received from my mother was well worth the memory of seeing this man tied to a tree with a bullet hole in one leg and an arrow, shot by a nine-year-old, in the other.

As I have said, in Africa, you do what you must to survive.

◇ ◇ ◇

IN 2000, THE OVERALL STABILITY OF THE COUNTRY NOSE-DIVED when President Robert Mugabe enacted "fast track" land reform, in which white farmers had a matter of months to relocate. Land reform wasn't something new to Zimbabwe. Even before its independence in 1980, when the country was known as the British colony of Rhodesia, land was a source of political conflict. After independence, there were tensions across all sections of society: between white landowners and Mugabe's government, between the government and the veterans of Zimbabwe's war of independence, and, less directly, between white landowners and an impoverished Black underclass. But as Mugabe's government was coming under criticism from all sides, he decided that a renewed call for land reclamation would solve a lot of his political problems. He opened the door for the radical redistribution of farms, giving the all clear to the war veterans to forcefully occupy desirable land. It was haphazard, disorderly, and violent.

I am not a political historian or an economist, and when this all began to happen, I was just a kid and simply recall the national atmosphere turning angry and chaotic. Suddenly, we had to drive to school with guns—and thank goodness. On two separate occasions, we had to fend off attackers who attempted to follow us onto our property. But more-forceful incursions had been succeeding all around us.

Ours was only a 200-acre farm. The farm to the west of us was one of the largest farms in Zimbabwe, comprising thousands of acres. In comparison, we were a speck. We were a tiny, high-end concern that produced fancy oranges, fancy avocadoes, and fancy flowers. We weren't harvesting millions of kilos of tobacco. Therefore, we weren't a primary target for "land reformers." However, any sense of our immunity quickly diminished one night in early 2002. By this time, the mdudu bike had become a well-known fixture on the farm, and I was riding the motorbike down to the dam on patrol when I heard gun shots. This could be my imagination—I cannot tell if I've made this up or if I actually perceived this—but I heard a bullet pass right by my ear, missing my head by inches. I looked up toward the neighboring fence line where approximately one hundred kids—for they weren't but a troop of teenagers with guns, on marijuana, and drunk as can be—were chanting, screaming, and firing at me. I got out of there on my motorbike as fast as I possibly could, zipping to the house, and told my mom, "The war vets are right on the fence. It's getting bad. They're getting close."

Although this policy of land reformation relied on pitting whites and Blacks against one another, we were no less African, and Africans don't flee. They dig in their heels and fight. All of our neighbors had done just that, and several of them were now dead; but it didn't matter to us, we would prepare and defend the farm. I was thirteen at the time, burdened with the responsibilities of a man, with no father to help, but still with boyish tendencies. And I was ready to go, armed, staring out my window, waiting for them to come, prepared to fight to the death. I find it hard to explain the reality of that mentality, its intensity, focus, and resignation.

The next day, having listened to their drumming until I fell asleep, I went to school, proceeding as normal, as you do in Zimbabwe. Toward the end of classes, my mother arrived early to pick us up, telling us, "Don't say anything to your friends, just come." Driving back home, she told me, "Everything's packed up, and it's time to go." I was furious, thirteen, and committed to dying for what was mine and what was right. My mother had spent the day gathering up our valuables and moving them to my grandparents' house. She told my sister and me that after we had gone to bed, a handful of the drunks from the fence line had fought their way up to the house and communicated, with their guns trained on her, that if we weren't gone by the following night, they would murder us all.

So be it, I thought. I was ready to fight, to die if I must, and said as much to my mother. Her rebuke felt like a slap: "You wish," effectively bursting any notion of heroic resistance. I got into the car with my sister. The three of us drove the half mile to the gate, and the fight within me turned to anguish. I cried as our dogs ran behind the car, chasing us to the road the way they always did. The farm workers' kids lined the drive. My friends, with whom I had spent a childhood marauding about the dam, knew we were leaving, and they waved. I would never see any of them again.

The dogs, the horses, the cows, everything, we left in an instant. We spent the night at my grandparents', but we weren't safe there. The recent elections were so charged with violence that all flights were overbooked, full of fleeing political refugees. After harrowing delays, we boarded the first flight out of Harare to London, where we stayed with cousins until we found our feet. When we arrived, we had US$400 to our names; because of foreign currency regulations, our

Zimbabwean currency was useless abroad. We stayed a few weeks there, in a state of limbo, my mother having intense conversations with our cousins, while my sister and I looked around ourselves for some sense of normalcy. As I often do, I went fishing, walking barefoot down the English streets to Hampstead Heath in my safari shorts. Having grown up in a former British colony, where white people were an extreme minority, there was something exciting about seeing all of these people who shared similar traits, customs, and qualities with the people I had known growing up. But instead of being hardened, grizzled, English Africans, they were these soft, delicate, London butterflies. I was no doubt an odd sight as I tromped across the manicured lawns of Hampstead Heath looking to catch native pike from one of its famous ponds. But our London layover abruptly came to an end when my mother decided to move us to California. I'm not sure where the money came from for the plane tickets, but there wasn't much left after we landed. I know our situation is a sight more comfortable than what many refugees around the world face today, but it was world-shattering to us. We had lost the life we had always known, our farm, our house, our friends, and our animals. We lost the beautiful and wild country of Zimbabwe, which, for all its dysfunction, was a setting made for adventure, for living to the fullest. And now the three of us found ourselves moving into a one-bedroom, public-housing apartment in downtown Oakland, California.

CALIFORNIA
DREAMING

CALIFORNIA DREAMING

As a family, we were in shock. We were crammed together in a small apartment, in a strange place, sharing items from the dollar menu. We were no longer safe not just in our farm, but also throughout the whole of Zimbabwe. We feared that my estranged father, in his jealousy and rage, could use his influence in government to ruin my mother—or worse, to imprison her. Had we stayed another night at our grandparents' home, we could have been detained by the police who appeared the next day, having been sent by my father. Instead, my mother's sister and her two-year-old daughter, who were visiting Zimbabwe from where they lived in California, were taken and held without cause in Chikarubi, a high-security prison considered the worst in the country. Prison in Zimbabwe is typically a one-way trip; but in this case, even the authorities, corrupt as they were, had to admit there was no reason to hold them. She and my cousin were released a few days later. The stress of all this drama, the intensity of disruption and uncertainty, was almost too much to bear for my mother, who suffered a pulmonary embolism after the flight from London to California. She was in the intensive care unit for a week and as she recovered over those following few weeks in California, I grew angrier and angrier.

Now, imagine me in Oakland, California, a white African boy with a funny accent, dressed in my smart shorts and button-down shirt, looking for an outlet, something to do, something that seemed normal. I'd see a bunch of kids, Black kids, playing basketball on a public court, and think, "Hey, they look like my friends from home. Let me see if I can get in this game!" I would run over, grab the ball, and try to start playing. This was never successful. They'd tell me to fuck off. They'd threaten me, surround me, and flash knives, and I was utterly perplexed. Where I grew up, if you wanted to play, you just joined in and moments later you were all having a good time. But not here. It didn't make any sense. No one wanted to be friends with me.

In Zimbabwe, if you and another boy had a disagreement or altercation, the teachers would tell you to go outside, sort it out, and come back in. You would walk outside, put your hands up, and have a go. One of you would get smashed in the mouth and wind up in tears. The other would head back to class, triumphant. Though, truthfully, half the time you would both end up in tears. This was how discipline worked. Once I was in the school system in Oakland, I applied the same approach to whoever was making fun of my accent that day. I kicked a lot of ass and got my ass kicked a lot, too. I was only fourteen but tough, angry, and unafraid of asking the school's eighteen-year-old starting linebacker to step outside. He definitely kicked my ass. For months, I would come home from school roughed up from fighting. I would constantly be in the principal's office, in trouble again. The whole time I just wanted to run away back to Africa, to live in the bush, to fight for my farm, to do things that were impossible.

When I wasn't fighting, I was running amok in Tilden Park, the "jewel" of the Berkeley park system. The park is full of Californian newts, *Taricha torosa*. Newts are a new world species and don't exist in Africa. I was fascinated and used to wade nipple-deep in the mud of this fancy park searching for amphibians, while prim San Franciscans decked out in North Face clothing stared at me. They must have thought I was deranged. But funny as it sometimes was, my mother understood that I was continuing to view the world through the lens of Africa—and it wasn't working. She knew that I needed a fresh start.

My aunt was now recuperating from her prison stint and told my mother that we could borrow her car. A newly found friend drove us to Los Angeles to pick it up. About halfway on the return trip, my mom headed west, wanting to follow Route 1 north along the coast. Soon after picking up the route, we crested a hill to see tiny Cayucos, California, coming into view. It was sunny, warm, nestled right on the Pacific Coast, and about as far away from trouble as you could get. With a town that had a population of 2,000, it felt more like an over-grown surfer encampment than anything else.

We turned onto Pacific Avenue to stop for lunch. While waiting for our food, we were spotted by a woman from South Africa—either we walked like Africans or my safari shorts had given us away—and she struck up what turned out to be a fate-ful conversation with my mother. Her name was Lesley Coma, and she invited the three of us to stay with her in Cayucos until we found our feet. My mom had already been thinking that this place was perfect. There was no way I could confuse anything in this Cali surfer town with anything in the African bush. It might just be different enough to get my mind on other things. And so, less than a week later, we had packed up our things in Oakland and drove back to Cayucos to move in with Lesley. We lived in her driveway, in a tiny camper situated on the bed of her pickup truck. My mom got a job as a hostess at one of the other restaurants in town. I was too young and too wrapped up in my own anger to understand how that must have been for her. But to go from being a renowned safari guide, an African bush pilot with your own plane, and an owner of a farm with 200 workers to hustling for tips in a small-town pseudo-Italian restaurant, all while raising two children, must have been devastating. Looking back on it now, she says, "It was as if someone had combined two movies, that of a struggling single parent and that of a refugee into a living nightmare."

I finished my last two years of high school in Cayucos. Our new home didn't change things overnight. I continued to fight and find new ways of getting into trouble. I remember confronting some eighteen-year-old creep who had been ogling my twelve-year-old sister at the skate park. I threatened him in front of the entire school, and he backed down. But, when I had my back turned, he sent me flying across the tarmac, ripping up my forearms, and then proceeded to deliver yet another beating with some older goon who had me physically overmatched. The cops showed up and arrested him. Later, I had my own police escort from one of Cayucos's two police officers. They had gotten into the habit of delivering me back home, where they would knock on our front door and greet my mother by her first name. Wisely, not long after we had arrived, my mother had launched a charm offensive against the local police force. She went to the station to explain our story and elicit help from the understanding small-town police. She would ask them over for dinner, bake them cookies, and do everything possible to keep them from throwing me into juvenile detention. But, despite all the official reprimands, I wasn't a bad kid. I never stole anything. I never broke anything. I was just from a different system, a place stuck in another era. So, when I'd bring a pocketknife to school, which is about as normal as carrying house keys in Africa, I'd end up in handcuffs. Or when I was arrested for drinking beer in public, I couldn't help but protest that all fourteen-year-olds drink beer in Africa!

As you might expect in such a small town, I was developing a reputation. Everyone knew that some feral African kid was now living there. I was often seen catching native gopher and king snakes in the surrounding scrub-covered hills or haggling for fish tanks at garage sales so I had someplace to keep those snakes. (Even though we were living between two places at the time, I still managed to re-create something of my old room in California.) It wasn't a surprise, then, when my mother received a call from a woman screaming about a fifteen-foot-long Burmese python that had eaten her cat. The snake was undoubtedly someone's escaped illegal pet. And the woman wondered whether I could possibly "come get rid of this giant snake!"

Now, I had caught rock pythons and cobras by this point, but I had never dealt with a fifteen-foot python before. This is an animal with serious brawn. But I showed up anyway, found the big snake in the bushes in the gully below the woman's house, and successfully identified the individual based on the cat-sized lump about a third of the way down its body. I caught the snake, brought it home, and built a cage out of scrap wood, wire, braces, and screws. I named him Willy-Eat-Me in tribute to his size advantage.

The story doesn't end there. That cat was only going to last Willy for so long. We had no money to feed him rabbits, so I decided that I would hunt for pigeons. I had come into possession of a Red Ryder BB gun, which was a step down even from a pellet gun and shot little steel balls. I dressed in camouflage (don't ask me why) and went down to the beach and then up a creek in search of my feathered quarry. But there weren't any pigeons at the beach or along the creek. I don't know why I thought there would be. As anyone knows, pigeons like to hang out on power lines. I abandoned the cover of the park to duck from bush to bush through a residential neighborhood, confident in knowing that my camouflage and stealth kept me completely hidden from prying eyes. I sniped one, two, three pigeons off a power line and felt proud of myself. I strapped the birds to my belt and crept back toward the creek, back down to the beach, and then up to my house. The moment I closed the door, proudly holding the three birds by their necks, a Black Hawk helicopter blasted by above the house. Then four cop cars came shooting down Pacific Avenue, Cayucos's one main street, where we have only two cops and one cruiser. Clearly, reinforcements were on the scene. Then, what seemed like five more helicopters were hovering in an aerial dragnet above our town. My mom turned on the TV, and the news was covering a terrorist alert in Cayucos, California, showing a far-off photograph of a man carrying a rifle, wearing camouflage, and walking from bush to bush near the town park. This was not a coincidence. My mom hid me underneath her bed until the National Guard response, which is what it was, finally blew over. They never did find the terrorist. My only worry is that telling this story will result in a large bill from the US government.

◇ ◇ ◇

BUT A BIG CHANGE WAS COMING. LIFE IN CAYUCOS WAS BEAUTIful in some ways and a struggle in others. And I still had my mind set on getting back to Africa, recovering our farm, and becoming a bush guide. There were no other considerations. For the time being, of course, I had to sit on my hands. I didn't have access to the kind of wildlife I had grown up with, so my enthusiasm found more-academic applications.

We did a lot of our shopping at garage sales, which is where I bought my first copy of the National Audubon Society's *Field Guide to Reptiles and Amphibians: North America*. Every time I acquired a new field guide, I would read it cover to cover. This is not something anybody does. It's a little bit like reading the dictionary straight through. I would read each guide three or four times, banking every species that existed in California; I was simply fascinated by all of these new animals. And it was at one of those garage sales where I made another seemingly modest purchase, but one that would set me on a path back to myself. Leaning in the back corner of this man's garage was a black fiberglass Hawaiian sling, also known as a pole spear. It was (and is—I still have it) a single black piece of metal with three prongs sticking out of one end and an old crusty dilapidated rubber band on the other. To use it, you loop the band around your hand, stretch it up to the top near the three-pronged spine, and release it, which shoots the spear forward at your target. I thought this was a tremendous piece of technology. I asked the man, "How much?" We settled on $1, still a significant purchase for me at the time.

A few days later, I borrowed a mask and a snorkel and announced to my mom and sister, "I'm going hunting in the ocean."

Now, I had grown up going to the ocean. Zimbabwe is a landlocked country, but my mother would fly us to Mozambique, three hours away, often with my grandfather, who loved the islands, diving, and spearfishing. She had set up a dive shop in the only lodge there in return for free accommodation throughout the year. When I was only a little boy, I snorkeled the reefs of the Mozambique Channel in the warm, tropical waters of the Indian Ocean. Central California is not Mozambique. It is not tropical, it is not warm, and it is not clear. But I took my $1 pole spear along with my ragtag mask and snorkel and went down to the fifty-two-degree water of the Pacific Ocean. We were north of Point Conception, so the water is freezing, not like in Southern California where you can actually swim. I had on my board shorts and remember the first time my face touched the Californian water with a mask on. It was so cold that I had an instantaneous ice-cream headache. It literally took my breath away. But the moment I had my bearings, I spotted a barred surfperch, and then a zebra perch, and then jacksmelt, opaleye, rockfish, lingcod, blenny, goby, kelpfish, and the list went on. I saw sea lions and seals. These large mammals swam past me to inspect or greet this uncommon visitor to their realm. And there was always the threat and the thrill of the possibility of a great white shark, which are most abundant in the waters off central California. Right in that instant, swimming within the rocking current, with life swirling all around me, I was transported back to the wild, back to the bush. I realized that as tame as California was above the surface, the second you got into the water, you were back in the food chain. At any point in time, a white shark could come rocketing out of the depths or a bull sea lion could charge. By the same turn, I could chase down a fish or grab a lobster. I can't say when exactly during that first dive it happened, but a switch had been flipped. All of my pent-up anger, pain, and longing to escape were gone.

This was my meditation. I was living in that moment and nowhere else. I had a huge smile on my face. I was thrilled to be back in a wild system and a food chain, all the while seeing new animals. I was hooked. I couldn't keep out of the water. After every dive, I would eventually emerge blue as could be, shivering, my lips purple, and then lie on the rocks like a lizard, as flat as I could get on the hot, jagged rocks in the sun, to warm up until my body would stop tremoring. And then I'd get straight back into the ocean again. I had found my wild.

◇ ◇ ◇

I AM NOT BY NATURE AN INTROSPECTIVE PERSON. MOST OF THE Africans I know aren't. But I think it would be fair to say that having gotten ahold of myself, having exited what felt like a freefall from my former life, I was steady again, and when you're steady, you can venture forth. And it was then that I benefited from a dose of life-changing luck that showed me the way.

Cayucos is tiny, but it isn't a secret, and it attracts other Californians who need a break from San Francisco or Los Angeles or, in the case of a vivid, beautiful, athletic, blonde-haired woman about my age, a respite from the studious life at a high school in the San Francisco Bay Area. I must thank my friend Alex Robinson, who unwittingly changed my life. His family lived next to a vacation rental house. Every summer, the same family, the Paneros, would rent that house. Their daughter, Lindsey, was this cute surfer girl that my friend Alex had eyes for. He was masterminding how to convince her to go on a date with him but was faced with the added complication that Lindsey had brought along her friend Jessica, an unwieldy third wheel that Alex needed to address. He called me up.

"Hey, Forrest. There's a really cute girl in the car named Lindsey and she's got this friend with her named Jessica."

I remember vividly the surf was firing that day.

"Cool, man," I said. "But I really don't care."

"No. Please. Forrest, listen to me," he said. "We can double date. You take this girl Jessica, so I can give my attention to Lindsey."

"I'm sorry, Alex. I just don't want to do that. The surf . . . I've got to get to it."

He begged some more. I remained adamant that I had to go surfing. Like I said, the surf was firing. Sensing that all his plans were close to falling apart, Alex put some money on the table.

"I'll pay you $20, and I'll pay for everyone's meals."

Twenty bucks was a lot of money to a fifteen-year-old surfer. A free meal was pretty appealing, too. So, I said yes. I met Alex and the girls at a little Mex hole-in-the-wall. He paid me the $20 up front to reimburse me for missing a day of surfing. As it would turn out, I'll be indebted to Alex until the day I die.

(Seventeen years later, Jessica and I are married and have a child. I don't think Alex ever spoke to Lindsey again after that date. It was the best $20 I ever made.)

On our double date, Jessica told me, "I'm going to the greatest school in the world! UC Santa Barbara. You should apply!" I had never heard of it. But she pushed through my ambivalence and showed me how college, rather than putting me on the path to some drab office-bound existence, could actually lead me to a life working with animals. She also became my girlfriend. She was persuasive.

Not much later, I visited the campus for a tour. I didn't have much hope that I would get into college. My grades were garbage. As soon as I had entered an American school system where you weren't beaten for not turning in your homework, I never did homework again. I couldn't find a reason to care. But fortune shined on me when I noticed a professor's collection of stick insects in his office. I didn't have an appointment. He had no idea who I was. But I walked straight in to discuss the many amazing things to know about stick insects, a lot of which was news to the professor. He took my mother aside to ask all about me and soon decided that I had something special. This professor, whom I encountered by chance, made sure I got into the University of California, Santa Barbara (UCSB), the only college I applied to, and helped to place me in the College of Creative Studies, a place for "radically curious" students.

Suddenly I was finding a new place for myself. I had Jessica, I had an academic future, and I was starting to find the people who shared my same passion for animals. For example, my buddy Nick Mancuso and I were the only two freshmen to petition to take an upper-division herpetology class. Apparently, we wanted our reptiles and amphibians and we wanted them now. But neither of us had bothered to check the email that said the first session was canceled. So, for fifteen minutes, we sat on opposite sides of an empty lecture hall, twiddling our thumbs, until Nick called out, "Dude, I don't think anyone is coming today." He ended up becoming my best friend freshman year, and we ended up planning an epic and unforgettable spring break. Now, when using the adjectives "epic" and "unforgettable" to describe a freshman's spring break, the destination is usually Señor Frog's in Cancun or Borgata in Las Vegas or a ski house in Lake Tahoe, and the intention is to rage and drink. Nick and I didn't have the funds for any such accommodations, nor the desire. What we had were a $25 tent from Big 5 Sporting Goods and backpacks. We didn't even have sleeping bags; we had bedsheets, which we took with us on a trip to the Ecuadorian Amazon. We flew to South America, sought out a canoe guide willing to take us, and had an absolute adventure wherein we caught twenty-one different species of reptile, including a twenty-foot anaconda. Nick became one member of an incredible peer group, who all breathed adventure and the outdoors, that I developed in college. Nick was the reptile guy. Jordan Machock was the land and tracking guy. Riccardo Dina was the fungi king (and today is one of the best mushroom foragers in California). And Adam Schewitz was my diving and spearfishing buddy. We each had our specialty and would come together for amazing trips all throughout college. We remain best friends to this day. And this is something to which I attribute much of my success, the good fortune to gather a like-minded group of individuals with complementary skill sets. It is the exact kind of dynamic I have with the crew of *Extinct or Alive*.

While a great group of friends can bring you a long way, so can a formal education. UCSB helped to channel my fervor for animals and being outside into an academic understanding of the systems at work in the field. It is true that I have had mixed feelings about school. I chafed under the strictness of the system in Zimbabwe. I floated through the lack of personal accountability in American high school. But, in college, never had my interests so perfectly aligned with my study, and there was absolutely no reason not to give it my all. I became a good academic scientist—which, I might add, is what sets me apart from most of the admirably insane survivalists you see on the Discovery Channel or Animal Planet. My academic background has often led directly to my success in tracking animals. Of course, UCSB didn't arm me with every fact I'd ever need to know, but it did teach me how to learn and how to interrogate new contexts, which is incredibly useful when searching for animals in places you've never been before.

But I made sure that my academic understanding developed hand in hand with my love of being in the field. Once again, my passion for snakes brought me to new places, this time to the office of the dean of the College of Creative Studies. I asked the dean if we could please create a class on field herpetology. And here is why the College of Creative Studies is such a magical place: he said, "Sure, and why don't you teach it, since you're the only one in this college who knows anything about field herpetology?" So, with the help of an academic advisor, I was now leading a field herpetology class every Thursday, when, for four hours, we'd target a group of species somewhere in Santa Barbara and go looking for them, all while learning about their ecology and habitat. It was a rare day when we didn't locate our target animal, whether that was the endangered western pond turtle, the Southern Pacific rattlesnake, or the California king snake. And while I led this course only for a single quarter, I realized how much students benefited from and loved field sciences, which, as a broke college student, got me thinking. If college students were paying tuition to learn about and look for animals, maybe I could offer the same experience to younger students, whose parents—especially in Santa Barbara, a hot spot for biodiversity as well as attentive parents—might be willing to pay for the kind of outdoor enrichment I was offering. And so, my business, Adventure Science, was born.

Parents would pay a monthly fee and their children could join me for weekly expeditions. At first, we started with tried-and-true turtles and rattlesnakes in Santa Barbara, but soon the expeditions were ferrying kids to the California Channel Islands to see foxes or collecting roadkill for dissection or snorkeling in rivers or exploring different chaparral zones. And this became super popular. Naturally led by my passion for reptiles and amphibians, I had gone from being a student, to a student-teacher, to an entrepreneur instructing employees and dozens of local school kids, ages five to fifteen, about science in the field. And despite my heavy course load, as well as my serious commitment to playing rugby, I managed to grow this business, which proved indispensable when it came time to graduate.

My grandfather had started a family tradition that when you graduated from college you received a round-the-world ticket. I guess back when my grandfather began the tradition, you could actually buy open-ended round-the-world tickets, which is what he did for his three children. Of course, my mother wasn't in any position to buy the airfare to fly me around the world, even though she was supportive of the idea. Instead, she helped me figure out how to make it possible. We sold my truck and my little boat that I'd purchased to take kids snorkeling. Together with the money I had made from Adventure Science and what my mom generously offered to make up the difference, I had my tickets that would see me through my first destinations. But I didn't leave right away. I waited for Jessica to graduate. I was a semester ahead because of how things worked out when I arrived from Africa. Compared to the United States, my schooling in Africa was rather advanced. I tested three grades ahead of my American peers, but my mother decided I should only place one grade ahead. But six months later, Jessica had financed her own travel by selling her car and whatever else she could. We packed our backpacks and planned a twenty-eight-country trip—or however many countries we could visit before we ran out of money. We jumped on a plane and wouldn't be back for another fourteen months, with negative $400 in our account and a brand-new vision for our life to come.

FINDING MY PATH AS A WILDLIFE BIOLOGIST

FINDING MY PATH AS
A WILDLIFE BIOLOGIST

Jessica and I headed west, which, for us, leaving from California, meant our first set of destinations included Samoa, Tonga, New Zealand, and Australia. We budgeted ourselves $50 per day and quickly became adept at asking strangers if they had a place for us to crash. We chose destinations where we could see wildlife that was on the verge of extinction. We sought out the rare and the dangerous, animals and places that might not exist ten years from now (and, sadly, many of them don't). From Australia, we continued to Micronesia, Vietnam, Laos, and others before embarking on an epic road tour of southern Africa, driving around Zimbabwe, Zambia, Botswana, Malawi, South Africa, and Namibia. Altogether, we visited twenty-eight countries, having an unrepeatable adventure.

We were tested by the whims of life abroad. We relied on the kindness of strangers and the quick thinking of our friends, and we created an inexhaustible trove of memories.

Those fourteen months away changed my thinking about our place on this planet and about the people in our lives.

We were in northern Thailand, embarking on an eight-day bush trek through its remotest regions. Accompanied by a troupe of fellow eco-adventurers, our guide led us to gorgeous waterfalls and caves, through miles of lush, mountainous, mist-sunk jungle. Every night we slept on the dirt and gazed up at the stars. But, aside from the incredible scenery, stars were just about all we saw. The jungle was quiet, the noise of birds overhead practically nonexistent, the buzz of insects muted. It was my first encounter with what has been described as "empty forest syndrome," which is especially prevalent in Southeast Asia. Humans had been hunting and harvesting for so long and so aggressively that they had depleted the jungle of its mammals, birds, and reptiles. Even the insects were affected by the imbalanced ecosystem. It was an uncanny feeling that I was unable to shake. We tried, though.

On the final day of the trek, we stopped at a thirty-foot waterfall about a three-hour hike from our extraction point. The season had been dry and the water was low, but it was still a glorious place to stop for a break. The girls in our group chose to lounge streamside. But, at the prompting of our guide, I clambered up to the top of the waterfall along with two Australian guys who were with us and jumped down into the pool below. All three of us raced up and down from the pool to the top of the waterfall three or four times each—it was as if we had a water park all to ourselves. But, of course, me being me, I couldn't do the same thing as everybody else, and jumping from the top of the waterfall was no longer good enough. I realized that underneath this falling curtain of water was a cavity you could climb into. My plan was to climb into the hollow and then jump through the downpour of water, bursting out the other side, a little bit like the Kool-Aid Man. The trick would be to clear the rocks at the base of the falls in order to reach the depths of the pool. I was more than confident that I could launch myself with sufficient force to land safely. So, being the cocksure twenty-one-year-old that I was, I scrambled up the slippery rocks and shouted down to my companions to say, "Everybody watch me, this is gonna be so cool." The ledge leading to the hollow was immediately beneath the curve of the waterfall, so still about thirty feet above the pool. I got into position and pushed off.

What I hadn't accounted for was that the water weighed thousands of pounds and was moving at an incredible rate, which, really, were the key factors in this equation. I did not break through to the other side. I was slammed straight into the rocks below, landing dead on my spine. Jessica saw the whole thing. I was not in pain. I felt nothing. I went from jump to splash to nothingness. From my neck down, I could do nothing and feel nothing. The crashing water pushed me off the rocks. I slid into the pool and started to drown. My hands, my feet, my entire body were useless as I drifted toward the bottom of this twenty-foot-deep pool.

Thirty or forty seconds passed with my eyes open in the murky, brown water, silently screaming at my body to, "Kick, kick, use your arms, swim." Then two arms plunged toward me, and someone grabbed me by the shoulders and lifted me toward the surface. It was Jessica, very much in the here and now. She dragged my inert body to the side of the river. I was paralyzed from the neck down and broke into tears.

"I can't feel anything."

She told me I would be okay. She held my hand and told me to hang on as others in the group cut down bamboo and vines to build a stretcher. My transport was ready in less than an hour, and I was carried the remaining miles to our extraction point, where a truck was waiting for us. They put me in the bed of a pickup truck and rushed me to the hospital that was about five hours away. On that ride, speeding toward my fate, I detached from all emotion. I went from crying to silent. Jessica rubbed my chest, reassuring me, encouraging me. But I had gone numb, physically and emotionally. I considered my life to be over. I couldn't reconcile my need to be outside and active with my likely future as a paraplegic. And I don't know whether to be ashamed of this or not, but I started to think of how I'd kill myself.

My despair was, thankfully, only temporary and lifted when, about halfway through the drive to the hospital, I managed to wiggle my big toe. All at once I realized I was going to be okay, just like Jess had been telling me. Riding the force of emotion that took me from thinking I was paralyzed to knowing I wasn't is something I will remember for the rest of my life. Over the next four or five days in the hospital, getting X-rays, fluids, and additional care, the feeling slowly crept up from my toes to my feet, my ankles, and upward, until I could actually move my legs. And as the ability to move returned, the pain arrived. I had fractured something in my spine that was pinching my nerve. Slowly, the swelling decreased and my ability to move returned. Soon enough, I was lying in the hospital bed, sore but recovered, amazed at how I could have progressed so quickly from nearly severing my spinal cord to preparing to continue on our trip almost as planned. The ordeal was so traumatic and yet the span of time so short, it was hard not to consider it a fluke, some blip in the normal flow of time—a lucky break, even. This memory reminds me of how some of my American crew members on *Extinct or Alive* react to surviving a close call—whether it's nearly stepping on a viper or staring down aggressive megafauna—wherein they turn inward and get hung up on what *almost* happened. A brush with death can make anyone squirrely. In contrast, and maybe it's my African upbringing, whenever I live to fight another day, I am simply stoked and ready for more. And that's how it was once I was up and walking again, signing out at the hospital, looking forward to whatever came next.

And sometimes what comes next is the end. Jessica and I were in Turkey not more than two months after my fall in Thailand. In that time, we had logged an incredible trip to Jellyfish Lake in Palau, a tiny nation in the western Pacific Ocean, where I traded the feeling of horrible nothingness with the feeling of bubbles—softball-sized, globular bubbles pulsating all around me. The lake was home to thousands and thousands of stinger-less jellyfish—nature's equivalent of swimming in *boba* tea—a perfect cure for an aching back. Now we had come to Istanbul, one of the few cities we visited. We were fourteen months and twenty-eight countries into our trip. After checking my bank account, I turned to Jessica and said, "We have negative $400 on the credit card and no money left in any of the accounts." She looked at me, paused for a beat, and uttered what I knew was coming, "Forrest, I think it's time to go home." That night we had the most expensive meal of the entire trip, putting us another $100 into the hole, and the next day boarded a plane to California, completely broke and the happiest we had ever been.

We returned with an incredible vision of wildlife and pristine habitats across the globe as well as with the realization that these animals and places were in trouble. I had been living in my beautiful, paradisiacal bubble in Santa Barbara, where wildlife was well-managed and you can see bobcats and coyotes on your way home from work, where white sea bass were making a comeback, great white sharks were returning, and sea lions were thriving in greater numbers than had been seen in one hundred years. That was not a microcosm of what was happening in the rest of the world or even the rest of the United States—everywhere else seemed to be dying.

I had seen firsthand the atrocities that were taking place: the habitat destruction, the loss of species. If I had had any reservations about being a biologist, about becoming a conservationist, the trip wiped them away. I knew I had to do something to make a difference on a global scale, because being a biologist in Santa Barbara, working with animals that were already recovering or counting species for management purposes, was not going to make a difference. That was all I knew. I didn't know how to do it or where to do it. But I knew I had to try, at the very least, to make an impact globally.

I decided I would make that impact as a wildlife biologist. I had the degree. I had the experience of seeing threatened and endangered wildlife in more than twenty-eight countries. I wanted to communicate science with passion, to share understanding for the cause of conservation. I had a grand mission. But, if you are beginning a career in biology—or in television, as I would unexpectedly find out—everyone starts in the proverbial mail room.

Fortunately, through UCSB, I was able to make a bunch of phone calls and knock on a bunch of doors and eventually connected with a former teacher's assistant of mine who gave me a job at his small biological consulting company. I was stoked. I thought to myself, "I'm gonna be a biologist! I've been an explorer. I've seen the Amazon and caught anacondas. I've had experiences no one else will ever have . . . I'm going to be running this place soon enough!" Typical freaking millennial. I was sure I was going to soar to the top. So, what was my first job? Well, it required me to wear a hazmat suit in 110-degree weather to pick weeds every day, all day. I was essentially hired to work as a very observant outdoor janitor.

Being a biologist is not tagging sharks and bald eagles and wrestling every rattlesnake in a given area. Your skills and education are most often applied to "grind work" such as habitat restoration. You must do the hard work of making a difference, one invasive weed at a time. I had to wear the hazmat suit because of the toxic chemicals I hauled around on my back to spray and pick weeds for months. Such was the glory of my new profession. I was still living with my parents, waking up pre-dawn, putting on this hazmat suit, mixing chemicals, and restoring riparian habitat. After months of pulling weeds, poisoning the ones we knew would grow back, and planting native species in their place, the company, which had been scratching by, started to grow, and I got the chance to work on the California Channel Islands.

The Channel Islands are the crown jewel of diving in California. All kinds of habitats from caves to kelp forests and all kinds of species from reef dwellers to oceanic travelers can be found there. The company invited me to work the contract. So, a week later, there I was, picking weeds in a hazmat suit on the Channel Islands, which was all the worse because I didn't have Internet access and couldn't sleep in my own bed. I lived in a low-fi research station on the center of Santa Cruz Island, without being able to dive or do any of the wonderful things the island had to offer.

Months passed at the research station, but real change was coming. The company informed me that I would be graduating from exterminating weeds to . . . counting ants, in this case, the invasive Argentine ant. While no one wants to work with weeds, I don't know if even ant biologists want to work with ants. They're not fun, unless you like trying to count roving specks. I am not exaggerating when I write that I counted 200,000 to 300,000 ants a day under a microscope. Again, months passed while I selected ant traps, counted the individuals, and determined how many invasive Argentine ants there were compared to how many native species. I repeat: 200,000 to 300,000 ants a day for months. I may be just that much crazier for the experience.

After the ants, I worked with rats, which are not native and were eating all sorts of things they weren't supposed to. I had to put cameras at potential nesting sites all over the islands, riding in boats and taking the occasional helicopter—all in the name of rat science! And after the rats came island foxes, a small, endemic species whose population had been decimated by the increasing number of golden eagles. So, you can see the progression here. I went from weeds to ants to rats to foxes, making gradual progress by showing up, doing good work, and keeping my goal in mind.

I was building a résumé as a biologist and eventually got to be a little choosier with the jobs I took, signing up for stuff that I loved, like working on banding western Pacific rattlesnakes. Whereas the other field technicians were catching two or three snakes a day, I was catching fourteen to twenty. I was wildly driven. I didn't have superpowers, but I would work double the time, starting three hours before I was scheduled and staying on five hours after my shift ended. I began to build a reputation in the local scientific community as a hard-working, high-risk wildlife biologist. Even when I was counting ants and picking weeds, I did so with some pep and enthusiasm.

So, one day, I returned home from the Channel Islands, covered from head to toe in limestone dust from the western-most peak of Santa Cruz Island, and, without even cleaning up, plunked down on the couch next to Jessica, exhausted. She had the television on and flipped to a channel where an overweight guy and a prim lady were standing naked in the jungle. They were talking into the camera, explaining the different ways they were struggling to secure food, water, and shelter while stuck in a remote location. We watched in silence for about ten minutes before I said something like, "What is this garbage?" Jessica explained, "It's called *Naked and Afraid*." We watched as the contestants moaned about having to perform basic survival skills, the kind of stuff that I did for fun. Jessica then ventured, "Maybe you should go on the show?" *Maybe I should*, I thought. I was burnt out from all my work as a field tech, and this seemed like a good chance for a break. After all, a holiday for me was usually some strenuous hiking trip with limited provisions anyway. So, I thought to myself, *why not get paid to do it for a change?* After finding out I could get a few weeks off, I wrote a horribly arrogant email to the production company. I don't have the email anymore, but it had a simple message: "Hey, my name is Forrest Galante and I am a lot better at survival than those people you're claiming as survival experts on your show." I never filled out an application. Ten days later I was on a plane to Panama to take on the *Naked and Afraid* challenge.

Now, I wanted to be a biologist. I didn't care about TV. I didn't care about getting fifteen (or fewer) minutes of fame. I viewed the experience as pure fun, as a vacation, as something new, because when are you ever going to run around the jungle naked for three weeks with a stranger? That's the attitude I carried through the twenty-one days of filming, which, of course, irritated the producers to no end, whose main objective was to capture pettiness and self-inflicted suffering on film. When I landed in Panama, I saw straightaway that I had a major advantage over the survivalists with whom I'd be taking on the challenge. I was the only trained biologist. I understood the ecosystem, habitat, and ecology. I was getting ready to live like a king, which is precisely what I did. I was eating 200 oysters a day. I was sunbathing. I mixed mushrooms with roasted lobster in a coconut bowl cured with citrus to make a heavenly jungle ceviche while everybody else was crying because they were in fact fake survival experts who had never learned a thing about the habitat they claimed to know how to survive in. I married all my wonderful field experience with my academic background and ended up as the most successful "survivalist" in *Naked and Afraid* history!

I could never write a book about proper bushcraft—how to build a fire, how to build a shelter, how to tan a hide. I can manage those things, but there are people who have developed those skills far beyond what I could achieve. A lot of those people have succeeded on *Naked and Afraid*, too. But if I were to boil down my advice on successful survival, it would be this: be adaptable and tenacious. You need to maintain a dynamic mindset wherein you look for opportunities within your given environment. Knowing how to start a fire, build a shelter, and hunt for game are important, but they are second-ary skill sets. They support the main objective of staying alive. And it is your mentality that will carry you through. It helps, sure, if you've studied biology and understand the natural sys-tems at work. Force of will can see you through, but a measure of familiarity with flora and fauna can make surviving a cinch.

After about a week or ten days into the show, we were on a jungle hike, having been told by the producer that we had to move so that different groups would encounter each other, and I stumbled upon an expanse of rich, dark soil and realized that it was a massive grove of yucca. Over the next fifteen min-utes, I managed to pull up thirty pounds of these giant, wild root vegetables, essentially gathering more food than anyone has ever had on the show and more food than anyone would ever need to survive twenty-one days in the wild. I was happy as a clam, threw the haul over my back, and walked off to our camp. Now, when I showed up with thirty pounds of food, the producers were pulling their hair out because my success was defeating the whole purpose of the show, which was to cap-ture as much human suffering and mewling as possible. But there I was with food, water, shelter, and a fire—everything in its place.

This is when the producers did something that surprised me. They threatened to take my food away. I was making things look too easy. I said to them, "Sure, go for it, and as soon as you leave me, I will go back to that yucca grove and by tomorrow morning, there will be another thirty pounds of po-tatoes there, and if you take that away, the next day there will be another thirty pounds of potatoes. And unless you know where that yucca grove is and you are going to destroy it, I'm going to feed myself like a king for the remainder of the show." I was not accepting their bullshit. I didn't care about making things work for the camera (something that my current crew members would say is still a problem); I was there to have fun. And, so, finally, the producers said to me, "Okay, do us a favor, just keep it off camera. We can't have you happy."

By the time the challenge ended, I had lost only twelve pounds, quite a feat when compared to the radical weight loss experienced by other contestants. I returned home, received compliments from Jessica about the weight I had lost, and three days later was back to my life as a biologist. The show wasn't going to change my world. I went straight back to work. Three months later, the episode aired. The producers had been adamant that no one was going to like me. They wanted me to change my attitude. They insisted that because I didn't cry or complain or tear down my partner, I was going to annoy viewers. But the opposite happened: I was a hit. I was goofy and happy-go-lucky as I ran around, catching oodles of food, building luxurious shelters, and catching snakes just because they were beautiful—unlike most terrified survivalists on the show who decapitated snakes for a measly meal without any knowledge of the beautiful animal they were killing. Instead, I talked to the camera about the reptiles, explaining what made them unique and pointing out the features that allowed them to thrive in their habitat, before letting them go. And watching myself those three months later, along with

4.5 million other viewers, admiring a snake and sharing that animal with others, I saw the first faint impression of a new path opening before me.

Three years earlier, when I published my undergraduate thesis about the effects of pollution on the downstream distribution of California newts, the paper received 400 reads by like-minded academics who already understood the subject matter. My television show, even though it wasn't mine, reached 10,000 times as many people. The math was simple and so was the message: if my goal was to change the world, then I had to reach as many minds as possible. Though the fieldwork I did—and that so many other scientists do—was valuable in terms of research and improving habitats, it wasn't going to make a big enough difference. I hadn't realized until that moment exactly what Steve Irwin had been up to. Like every other kid I knew, I loved watching him lose his marbles over a lizard or a giant croc. But it hadn't occurred to me that he was purposefully communicating his enthusiasm and love for animals through television to grow or encourage that passion in others.

Although I have sometimes been dismissed as "just a guy who got famous because he was on *Naked and Afraid*," to which I quickly reply that hundreds of other contestants have appeared on the program, and I'm the only one with his own award-nominated television series, I credit the show with introducing me to what TV can do. Like everyone else who's ever been on, for exactly one week after the episode aired, I had my five minutes of fame. Reporters from local newspapers—think the *Santa Barbara Press*—called me up. A typical conversation would start like this:

"Hey, what was it like on *Naked and Afraid?*"

"No thanks."

"No thanks? What do you mean, 'No thanks'?"

"It was just a show I did for fun. I don't wanna talk about it," and just as they were about to hang up, I'd say, "But I'll tell you something I will talk about . . . "

"Ok, what's that?"

"I'll tell you about the hammerhead that I found in the California Channel, the first hammerhead to have been spotted there in twenty-five years. I'll tell you about the 11.8-pound lobster that I caught, one of the biggest ever taken in the state of California. I'll tell you about the rattlesnakes that I'm banding and how rattlesnakes are a good thing for the environment and why we need them in the world. We do not need another story about some loser who walked around naked on TV."

About half of the reporters said, "No thanks," click. And about the other half said, "Yeah, okay, I guess. Tell me more about blank."

So, I started telling them stories about conservation and wildlife in our own backyard in California, and a couple of those stories went viral. The video of me catching this giant lobster and taking him to an aquarium because I couldn't bring myself to eat him, and then releasing him in a national park, received millions of views. The video of me getting chased around by a hammerhead had people going nuts, even though it was some shoddy film caught on my buddy's GoPro while we were spearfishing. As a result of the positive reception, more reporters started to contact me, and I told them more stories—about traveling the world with my girlfriend, about the rare animals we encountered—and shared my photographs. These stories gained traction, too, which provided a valuable lesson: had I just gone along with those reporters who wanted to talk about my turn as a reality TV show contestant, those stories would have run and a week later that would have been it. I'd have gone back to working as a field technician. But I pulled the focus to what I cared about, even if I had to be confrontational about the point I was making, and eventually I found out that other people cared about it, too.

This media snowball didn't happen all at once. The stories and the videos appeared over the course of more than a year after my adventure in Panama. But word continued to travel, and I started hearing from talent agents at all the big agencies. And I flat-out told them, "No, I'm not stupid. You're all used car salesmen trying to make a quick buck off of my fifteen-minute window. I don't want a manager." I didn't like their approach and laughed out loud while turning them down—until one guy, not much older than me, genuinely seemed like a nice guy. His name was Alan Moore, and he told me, "Fair enough, you don't need an agent, but let me introduce you to a guy who I think you'll like. His name is Patrick DeLuca. He's your age, maybe a bit older, and he loves wildlife the way that you love wildlife." I wasn't buying that, but he continued. "It's true, he was a producer on *Whale Wars*, has always wanted to film wildlife, and is looking to create his own concept."

Finding My Path as a Wildlife Biologist

I agreed to meet Patrick but requested that if he was serious, he would need to meet me in Santa Barbara, not Los Angeles. To his credit, he did, and a few days after speaking with Alan, I got a call from Patrick, who trotted out the showbiz gem, "Let's do brunch." At that point, my heart was still set on continuing a career as a wildlife biologist. I wanted to find ways to share my passion, sure, but I didn't think I wanted to work in television. So, when Patrick asked where we should do brunch, to test his commitment, I suggested the Biltmore, which is a Four Seasons Resort in Santa Barbara and way outside either of our price ranges. He didn't balk, though it wasn't entirely clear who would be picking up the bill. I brought Jessica, he brought his girlfriend, it was $150 per person at minimum, and we proceeded to have an extravagant lunch that no one could afford, with lobsters, oysters, and rounds of mimosas. Patrick told me later that he had no idea how he was going to recoup his losses. I had yet to throw myself behind the idea of developing a television show, but there is something to be said for $25 mimosas. As the brunch rolled on, we started evolving this idea we were calling "Hunting Lazarus," which referred to the biblical story of Lazarus, who came back from the dead. The idea was to pursue and maybe even find animals that people had given up on and for which nobody was funding a search. We emphasized that these were *real* animals, not Bigfoot or anything else on the cryptozoology wish list. It was important to draw the distinction when talking to television executives, who have a long and successful history of running shows wherein the hosts never find what they are looking for.

The brunch was overpriced but fateful. Patrick walked away with a solid pitch and my okay and took the idea to market.

Then what seemed like every production company in Los Angeles told us, "No." In person, over the phone, on Skype, Patrick and I pitched the idea for weeks and dug in our heels against the unrelenting torrent of rejection. "Not interested." "That's stupid. You'll never find the animal." "Don't waste my time. Neither of you have any experience. Neither of you have any credentials in television." Etc. So, I hopped on a plane to New York City, expecting more of the same, but not willing to let the idea die. I walked into a few different production companies, totally blind, and (thanks to Alan Moore) eventually wended my way to Hot Snakes Media on Broadway, all the way downtown by Trinity Church. I asked if I could meet the owner, and the kind receptionist said, "Sure." A man named Eric Evangelista welcomed me into this office. He was very curt, all business, and asked, "What do you want?" I rolled into my pitch, which had become fairly well-honed after our experience in Los Angeles, and he listened quietly and patiently and then said, "Okay. Let's give it a try." I must have gawped at him a moment, because he gave me a look that clearly conveyed, "Got it. Now get out of my face," which I was totally happy to do.

That's all I needed. I walked out of that office and told Patrick that we were partnered with Hot Snakes Media. But now I was truly facing a fork in the road. My pursuit of the television show was almost quixotic; I had approached the possibility in the same way I approached *Naked and Afraid*, as in, let's have some fun and see what happens. Now it was happening, and I had to make a conscious and careful decision about where I wanted to focus my time and energy, where I wanted to direct my life, and whether I was okay with walking away from what had been my practically predestined path of becoming a working wildlife biologist. Complicating matters, the more traditional academic path was throwing roses at my feet, if you could call $70,000 per annum plus benefits roses, which most of us would. But a real biologist spends 90 percent of his or her time in an office, sitting at a desk; staring at a computer; and writing grants, papers, and survey reports. Any time the prospect of such a job came up, I kept declining, citing the reasons above and telling them I'd rather work as a tech. "But," they'd reply, "a tech only makes $14 an hour." They sure do, but they're also outside contributing, making a physical difference in the environment. Their hands are dirty on the snake, on the fox, on the weed. I didn't want to write reports, even if that meant limiting my potential advancement in the field. Now that *Hunting Lazarus* was more than drunken brunch talk, I viewed the show not just as a rare opportunity to make television, but as a means to work in the field and make the kind of impact I had been dreaming of.

Eric, who has since become one of my best friends (he's a remarkable man), then took the project to the networks for his own round of pitching. And as before, the "no"s came rolling in, as plentiful and unstoppable as the tide. But, finally, from Animal Planet, the house that Steve Irwin built, we received a "maybe." For six months after that maybe, we worked on the scripts and the decks, writing upwards of a gazillion emails, strategizing on the phone for countless hours, and doing everything we could to turn that maybe into a yes. However, when the yes came, it was more of a, "We'll give you one chance." Animal Planet signed us up for what is known as a "backdoor pilot," which is a pilot disguised as a one-off special. If the special performs well, then the network might turn it into a series.

With one more major push, with a true proof of concept, we could get our series, and *Hunting Lazarus* would have its first birth. I was driven not by the prospects of fame or fortune—and I truly hate to break it to you that you don't get rich making television—but by the ability to finance traveling around the world, picking up where Jessica and I had left off in Istanbul, to chase down rare and exotic species and to share that wildlife through Animal Planet. There was just one condition, however. (There always is.) Animal Planet would run the special but only during "Monster Week." So, I told them no.

A MONSTER WEEK

A MONSTER WEEK

Monster Week was Animal Planet's answer to Discovery Channel's Shark Week (more on that later). The shows range from Bigfoot hunters to megalodon fetishists to animal attacks. I told Patrick and Eric that we weren't looking for monsters. We were searching for real animals that had been pushed past the brink, or maybe not, by the abuses of civilization. Our concept didn't fit along with the others. I was never afraid to say no to something that didn't feel true to my vision, so why should this be any different? It had worked to my benefit several times in the recent past. But Patrick and Eric talked me off the ledge. They helped me to realize that not every situation is black and white, there isn't always a moral line running down the middle of an issue, and there were times when a compromise is strategic and will ultimately serve a larger purpose. Plus, Patrick and Eric had been working their brains out for just this opportunity, and they weren't going to let me blow it. So, I held out hope that the pilot would go well and that our show would ditch the monsters at the first opportunity.

At some point while preparing our special, we dropped the title *Hunting Lazarus*, opting instead for the now familiar and more to the point *Extinct or Alive*. The first species we planned to search for was an aspirant member of the Lazarus taxon, a poster child of extinction, the thylacine, also known as the Tasmanian tiger.

The Tasmanian tiger was a carnivorous marsupial that looked a lot like an elongated dog, with dark stripes running down its haunches, and was famous for the uncanny gape of its jaws. The last known individual died in 1936 in Tasmania. There was plenty about the animal for Monster Week to love, but I was excited simply to have our chance to search for the animal. Its historic range included Australia and Papua New Guinea. Maybe somewhere in that extensive landscape there was still a surviving population, but we focused our efforts on finding the animal in Tasmania, a smaller but not insignificant landmass 150 miles off the southeast coast of Australia. And right as we finalized the plan to fly a film crew—along with an absurd amount of equipment—across the world, terrible fires broke out across the Tasmanian backcountry, effectively canceling what would have been my first step toward promoting conservation on television. Or, anyway, the network wanted to cancel it. Most productions shut down in the face of wildfire, but I made a strong argument to the contrary.

While my team was groaning that all our work was for nothing, I got everyone from the network on the phone to make the case that the fire was in fact an opportunity. We would use it to our advantage. Their immediate response was, "Dear God, no. You will not do that. Not only is there no advantage to be gained but it will be an insurance nightmare. The fire could pop up anytime, trapping all of you. Game over." But I refused to cancel the expedition. As the wildlife biologist on the project, I asked everyone to trust me. I showed how we would scour maps of the rugged area we had been planning to search, assessing wind direction, to locate two parallel mountain ranges that were positioned perpendicularly to the path of the burn. Every animal in the area would be funneled down into the central valley. I proposed that we would set up our base camp at the end of the funnel, effectively catching a massive concentration of animals fleeing the fire. If thylacines were anywhere in the area, they would be among the thousands of animals moving through this choke point of escape. The irresistible logic of this argument did practically nothing to convince the network that it was a good idea. But I would not relent. We found the ideal location on the map. We argued for the chance for great television as well as for a potential discovery. And eventually the network was comfortable enough with our comfort in putting ourselves at risk that the production could continue.

We flew the crew to Tasmania, set up our camp, met up with Nick Mooney, a preeminent biologist there, and watched as thousands upon thousands of animals surged down the valley ahead of the flames, all headed in the same direction, right on the path I had predicted. Wombats, wallabies, quolls, Tasmanian devils—all sorts of incredible species were on the march. And amid this remarkable parade of survival, we failed to identify a single thylacine. Maybe we missed them, but that wasn't likely. We had no trouble spotting all the other animals after all. And our dragnet of cameras efficiently canvased the limited area through which the wildlife was passing. The thylacines simply weren't there.

The lack of a positive identification was to be expected. The shoot didn't last long. We would have been foolish to have been hopeful that we'd overturn nearly a century of scientific consensus after just two weeks of investigation. But I had proven something nevertheless. Those animals showed up right where I expected them to. If thylacines had been there, we made pretty good odds for ourselves that we would have spotted them. Suddenly the idea of dropping into an unfamiliar location, even someplace vast and remote, to perform an effective search was not as outlandish as it had first seemed.

I returned home and resumed life as a working biologist, waiting for the show to air without any clear idea of how it would be received. Once again, I had pushed back against the producers' expectations. We didn't showcase the thylacine as a monster, but as a fascinating predator that got into trouble when preying on livestock. We discussed how it was undeservedly driven to extinction. I never crawled into my tent, shaking and whispering into the camera about the likelihood that I would end up a midnight snack for prowling Tasmanian tigers. And I intentionally never filmed anything that could be edited into standard Monster Week content. The network worried the show would be a mismatch for the week's otherwise pulpy programming and ran it in an unfavorable time slot. And yet *Extinct or Alive* was a huge success. We didn't show viewers the Tasmanian tiger, but we offered them a rare glimpse into a fascinating ecosystem. We even topped Jeremy Wade's *River Monsters* special in the ratings, which no show had been able to do for years.

Patrick, Eric, and I were ecstatic and proud of what we had done. We thought, *This is it. This is our launching point to begin a series of showcasing wildlife around the world.* I had wanted to find a way to make a global impact. My goal was never anything less than that. And now I was on the verge of having a platform that would regularly share my message with millions of viewers. Because our thylacine special was such a success, we naïvely presumed that the executives at Animal Planet would quickly green-light the series. It would be a no-brainer. We waited for the good news to arrive. And we waited. May turned into June, summer turned into fall, and we had no word about the network's decision. My contract was set to expire on December 31 of that year. Then, on Christmas Eve of 2014, having not received any communication from the network for seven months, having given up hope that the series would happen, and thinking that Animal Planet just didn't care about extinct animals, I received an email with a single line of text: "Congratulations. You have yourself a series."

It was the best Christmas present I have ever received.

◇ ◇ ◇

I HAD MY WORK CUT OUT FOR ME.

Up until this point, I had managed to produce a single pilot. Even though I didn't know what I was doing, I was able to focus on and execute a single concept. Now, to create the first season of *Extinct or Alive*, I had to produce eight episodes of comparable scope and complexity and had to plan them all at once. The size of the task was a shock to the system, but it was sink or swim.

Patrick and Eric turned to me and said, "Now what?" They weren't wildlife or extinction experts. So, my first task was to come up with the list of potential animals to search for. The pool of possibilities was extensive. But the animals I chose needed to not only potentially still exist but, despite scientific consensus to the contrary, they needed to be charismatic or compelling enough to carry an hour of television. I wasn't going to be following up on reports of extinct snails showing up in someone's garden (even though I'd be ecstatic for that particular snail). There needed to be a story with some punch that would be an easy sell to viewers. So, if you're looking into the white wolves of Newfoundland, which were hunted to extinction because of a bounty placed on their heads by settlers and now the Canadian government was covering that up, and if a remnant population might still exist thanks to a remote land bridge leading into the Labrador forest, now you've got a story to sell. And though we weren't looking for snails, we weren't looking for anything that died out earlier than the industrial revolution. The show wasn't a stunt in which I went looking for dinosaurs. We pulled together this Rolodex of fascinating animals that could still exist, wherein we could explore the question: Why has the whole world got it wrong?

And there I was, Forrest Galante, a biologist who was counting ants nine months ago, advertising that I was the one who was right. Talk about painting crosshairs on your back. I was a lone biologist from Santa Barbara who was calling into question whether a giant organization like the International Union for Conservation of Nature (IUCN), which was the authoritative body that declared whether a species was extinct, had gotten things wrong. This was David and Goliath stuff in the world of conservation. To some, my willingness to challenge the powers that be was a show of arrogance. To others, my openness to the possibility that these species might still exist bordered on the clownish. But if you're going to change the world, you're going to hear all the reasons you can't or shouldn't. As Charles Darwin famously posed, "If you had an idea that was going to outrage society, would you keep it to yourself?"

We kept our focus on the species and reviewed our criteria: When did the animal go extinct? Who declared it extinct? Why was it declared extinct? Is there enough habitat left where the animal used to live? Is there enough prey source or food availability for that animal, if it still existed in lower numbers? Is there a remote-enough region? And then, what evidence is there that this animal might still be alive? In other words, who's looking? Who's had sightings? Who's reported seeing one or killing one or hitting one with their car? And this isn't information that just pops up on Google. Think about it: if you're driving one night and happen to smash a turtle on the freeway, you're not going to pull over, walk back toward the animal, and determine that, "Oh wow! It's a critically endangered diamondback terrapin. I need to post about this!" That's not happening. You're still driving home, hoping that your tires are okay.

Research was obviously a big part of the job. I was on the phone for days and days on a relentless search for information. It was a little bit like when I went around to production companies and pitched the idea of the show. By and large, there was nothing to be found, but, occasionally, a glimmer of information came to light. As we searched for clues, we had to factor for each animal's known ecology—when is it feeding, when is it mating, when is it out and busy? We had to plan around seasonal climate—when are there monsoons, typhoons, torrential rains, fires? We had to predict how the animal's ecology would align with those environmental factors in order to optimize our chances of success. And we had to puzzle together eight expeditions, one after the other, so that travel and timing would support the possibility of finding the animals we were after.

Not only did I have to string together a series of successful trips but I had to account for complex ecological factors in each location. For example, the Formosan clouded leopard, which hasn't been seen in twenty-five years, mates in late spring. If you go too late in the season, you run into the monsoons. If you go too early, the animal isn't out yet and won't respond to calls. So, presuming that the animal isn't extinct, you have a five-week window to potentially encounter the animal, and that's it.

The forty-four minutes of television you watch (with sixteen minutes of commercials to round out the hour) is essentially a distillation of years of research, months of planning, and weeks in the field. But we make the effort because we care about finding the animal. We care about inspiring people about conservation, and we hope the species and ecosystems featured on the show will benefit from increased awareness.

Our completed calendar had the same look and feel as John Nash's calculations in *A Beautiful Mind*. Compared to whatever it takes to film Kim Kardashian texting at a hair salon, the amount of work that went into each and every episode of *Extinct or Alive* was insane. Eventually, we put together a list of eight animals: the Formosan clouded leopard, the Newfoundland white wolf, the Florida black panther, the great auk, the Pachylemur, the Javan tiger, the Tasmanian tiger (round two!), and the Zanzibar leopard. Each expedition would last anywhere from two-and-a-half weeks to a month.

Even with our best-laid plans, there were only obstacles. For example, I had absolutely no idea how to make television. Not really. I had never operated a video camera in my life. I didn't know what OTS (that's an over-the-shoulder shot) or

ITM (that's an in-the-moment interview) meant. I didn't know the difference between 4k and 1080 and 720 vertical resolutions. I didn't know what frame rate to use. I knew nothing, and, at least in the early episodes, I was okay with that. I had no interest in what the show would look like. (That has all changed, of course.) Realizing this, Patrick and Eric put together a small crew to help me. They were an audio guy, a showrunner, two camera operators, and an editor in the field. I had a few phone calls with these guys to explain the goal of the show and how the show would be run (by me), but I met them all for the first time at the Los Angeles International Airport (LAX) on the eve of our search for the Formosan clouded leopard. I was attired in rugged, quick-dry field clothing and hiking boots and they were slouching around in skinny jeans, backward caps, and Lululemon T-shirts, looking all sorts of LA. I thought to myself, "Oh boy, I don't know how this is gonna go." One of this original bunch flamed out horribly on the first expedition. And only one, Mitchell Long, still works with me today, having survived everything this show could throw at him for multiple seasons. Mitch was one of the camera operators and looked as LA as anyone, but he's proven to be an absolute rock in the field and has become one of my best friends in the world. But that's now. Back then, I was a pain in his and everyone else's backside.

I didn't behave like the typical host who followed instructions on where to stand, what to say, and where to look. My focus was on the animal, not the camera. So, whenever they asked me to slow down, redo a shot, or repeat myself because audio wasn't ready, I was not very understanding. My job was to find an animal that hadn't been seen in decades, if not longer, *in two weeks*, and I didn't have time to care about the niceties of film production. I wanted to find the animal and that was it. It took time for me to appreciate the obvious fact that finding an animal is not making a television show, and my job was to do both. So, while I found it extraordinarily frustrating that I had to turn to the camera to say things like, "I'm doing this because of this. I'm here to do this because this is how this animal works or thinks. This animal's biology dictates X," it was mission critical to the point of the show. As the host, I couldn't keep information to myself. I had to learn (and am still learning) how to present key information, in everyday terms, so viewers could understand and thus appreciate the biology at work. I also had to check the impulse, which is sometimes impossible, to take off sprinting after an animal, giving the cameraman only a shot of the back of my head.

I loosened my grip not only because I would have had a mutinous crew on my hands but because facing down extinction will quickly reset your expectations. The sad fact was that no matter how hard I worked or how intensely I analyzed the data, the animals I was looking for weren't right around the next corner. They were gone from the face of the earth. And even if they weren't, the odds of me being able to find an animal that hadn't been seen in ten or twenty or one hundred years within a window of two to four weeks were zero. This knowledge played in the back of my mind throughout the first season of *Extinct or Alive*. If you gave me two weeks to find a great white shark in California, a place where we know they live all year long, I probably couldn't do it. And that's a common and very large animal.

I realized that my primary goal was to share my passion for conservation, so emphasizing only the success or failure of the search was counterproductive. Those camera talks were more than just a tool of television; they were my way of inviting viewers into the journey, into the jungle, the mountain, the reef, the cave, or wherever we happened to be searching. They were my way of sharing my wonder for wildlife—its diversity and adaptability, its form and function. If *Extinct or Alive* was going to be more than some high-minded redux of *Searching for Bigfoot*, if it was actually going to inspire kids to get into science, then the journey itself would need to be worth the price of admission. The destination—the resurrecting of an animal that the scientific community had, with great finality and for good reason, declared extinct—was almost too beautiful to think we'd ever get there.

But then we did.

REWRITING NATURAL
HISTORY (THE FIRST TIME)

REWRITING
NATURAL HISTORY
(THE FIRST TIME)

The road to discovery was long, arduous, and twisting. Filming the first season of *Extinct or Alive* was a challenge and a learning experience, but it also filled me with a strong sense of purpose. Although we weren't tripping over extinct animals wherever we went, we were highlighting beautiful environments and urging the viewer to care about protecting what was left. I knew we would succeed on that front, but, as a scientist, I didn't have any kind of blind faith that we'd actually discover one of our target species.

There was plenty to distract me from that sobering reality. Our first expedition took us to Yushan National Park in Taiwan, a lush remnant of what the island nation used to look like, and potentially the home of the Formosan clouded leopard. And although I met passionate scientists and trekked through beautiful terrain, where Mitch was nearly bitten by a "hundred-pacer" (if you're bitten, you walk a hundred paces and then you keel over dead), my showdown with an armed and drunk porter will probably be what I remember most. If you've watched the episode, you'll know that the porters, locals we hired to transport our equipment to camp, planned to hunt while we filmed. I repeat: they planned to hunt in a national park while working on a conservation show and had brought a gun with them. The episode depicted some of my frustrations, but we stopped filming when I wrestled a porter to snatch his gun away from him. I got the gun, which, luckily, wasn't loaded, and kicked him off the job. This was considered culturally insensitive by my hosts and my producers, but I could not give a damn. Wasn't I supposed to be searching for a leopard? Instead, I was finding poachers on my own team. It is no wonder animals are driven to extinction.

But charismatic fauna of the living variety caught my attention, too, like when I traveled to Australia for a second attempt to find the thylacine. I had an incredible time working with researchers from James Cook University, but my unplanned encounters with a cassowary and a taipan proved that the life of a wildlife biologist can get exciting quickly. Often referred to as the "world's most dangerous bird," a cassowary is not to be trifled with and can seriously wound if not kill you. They also look like beautiful, modern-day dinosaurs. They have a hard crest on top of their strikingly blue heads. Their body is covered in dense, bushy feathers and their long, sturdy legs end in lethal-looking feet. I had wanted to see one my whole life. We were filming near a promising water source when two individuals, an adult and a juvenile, moved through the understory toward us. For a tense moment, their behavior was hard to predict, and I had to intervene to distract the adult from potentially harming a crew member. But once their feeding brains turned back on, they stalked away, leaving us all with an image of just how wild this world can be. My attempted rescue of a seven-foot-long coastal taipan wasn't nearly as serene.

I have playfully disparaged the lethality of Australia's animals in comparison to those of Africa's. And I stand by it. But the taipan is a big reason Australia has the reputation it does. We were getting an eyewitness report from an old Aboriginal man in a tiny village about a thylacine sighting from ten years earlier when we heard screaming—truly crazy screams of panic—and I dropped the interview and ran to see what was happening. A man was holding a cinder block above his head, aiming to smash something moving through the grass. His intent was to smash a taipan. Although taipans have an extremely neurotoxic venom that attacks your nervous system and clots your blood, it doesn't mean they deserve to die. But I understood the villagers' panic. From their view, unless they killed the taipan, it would kill one of them. And so, I launched into my taipan-rescue mission, which could have easily become a Forrest-rescue mission. I ran in front of the man, telling him to, "Stop, stop, stop," to the point where he almost smashed *me* with the cinder block. I pulled out my flimsy little snake hook and the taipan shot under a house. I assured everyone that I would get the snake out of there. I belly crawled under this building, which was raised on cinder blocks about twenty-four inches off the ground, trying to locate and remove a snake that is the third most venomous in the world. It was pitch-black under the building. Even when I used my light, I couldn't see a thing. I was telling my crew, "I don't see it, I don't see it," when it slithered over the back of my neck, trying to escape. An aggressive and fired-up taipan had me dead to rights. I froze as best I could because I knew if I freaked out or twisted, it would have latched onto my neck, and that would have been the end. A bite from a coastal taipan will turn your blood black. To this day, as I type these words, the memory gives me goose bumps. It was a bone-chilling and awful experience to have been utterly exposed like that. Five minutes later it bolted from its hiding place and I helped move it off the property.

Throughout the making of season one, I had incredible experiences. We came close to verifying the existence of the white wolf of Newfoundland, having met a man who'd shot one. We recorded a compelling thermal signature of what could have been a Javan tiger in Indonesia. But we hadn't found any extinct animals. With our storytelling, we challenged the notion that extinction was final just because a governing body such as the IUCN said so. But we hadn't done anything to back up our position or prove anyone wrong, and it all came down to the very last expedition in Zanzibar.

Rewriting Natural History (the First Time)

On our first flight out of LAX, on our way to Taiwan, I was seated next to Mitch. It was the first time we had met. He asked me, "Of all the episodes, Forrest, on which one do you think we're most likely to find the animal?" My response was something like, "I wouldn't count on us finding any of them. There's always a remote possibility, but I wouldn't get your hopes up." Mitch then asked, "Of all the episodes, which one is the least likely that we would find the animal?" Without pause, looking him dead in the eye, I answered, "Mitch, there is no hope in hell we'll find the Zanzibar leopard." I told him it was a tiny island with more than one million people living on it. The national park was less than twenty square miles. "The only reason we're going," I continued, "is because it's such a fantastic story of contradiction, of wildlife and witchcraft. Even though I have some evidence, we're never going to find that animal."

Fast forward eight months and we were in Zanzibar, off the coast of Tanzania, meeting with local anthropologists, not even biologists, to review reports of some goats being mutilated. The photos they showed me could have been the work of a leopard, or a dog, and there were thousands of stray dogs on the island. We then headed to Jozani Chwaka Bay National Park, the island's only national park, to the site of the goat killings, which were adjacent to this last, surviving patch of wild habitat. It was the first time we had encountered a natural environment on the island. We were moving away from the dense towns and surrounding farms. We arrived there right at sunset, and the forest was coming alive with lightning bugs, unseen animals scurrying in the undergrowth, and the incessant noise of insects. It was a small park, but it felt like the real bush to us. Compared to the silence of the town, noiseless except for human activity, Jozani was deafening. We realized that even in this little pocket of habitat, wildlife was flourishing. It always does when given half a chance. But, just as the spell of the forest was descending upon us, the *adhan*, the Muslim call to prayer, sounded from speakers in the nearby village, filtering through the trees and foliage, reminding us that civilization was only a stone's throw away.

We were blessed by the local witch doctor, who told us how long ago the island's witch doctors used to keep the leopards to do their evil bidding. He viewed the animal as a spiritual avatar that could intervene in the affairs of humans. But, he said, "They're gone. We don't use them anymore." We traveled to a museum to view a specimen of the leopard, which went extinct roughly twenty years earlier. It was beautiful. But, while we were learning about a fascinating culture and an unusual dynamic between humans and wildlife, there was no definitive proof that the leopard was still alive. All signs were pointing to no.

Word must have traveled that a foreigner was looking around for an obviously extinct animal. The evening after our visit to the museum, a man approached me outside of our hotel. He told me that he knows a man who lives on the northern part of the island, who keeps a Zanzibar leopard in his village. This seemed like just the kind of break I would need, since we had already visited the national park and the size of the habitat just didn't seem promising. The man said he would show us the way in exchange for an exorbitant amount of money. For lack of a better option, I proposed terms. "Here's what I'll do. I'll give you US$100 today. When you show me the leopard, I'll give you $100 tomorrow."

I grew up in Africa. I have traveled the world. I've had AK-47s pointed in my face while people have politely requested bribes. You'd think I would have known better than to hand someone $100 and say, "Sure, please show me the extinct animal now." But I did not. Of course, we traveled to the village, and no one there had ever heard of the guy. He had vanished with $100, which wasn't the end of the world, but nobody likes getting robbed. So, the search was not going well. It seemed as if the entire first season of my show was going to land squarely in the "extinct" column.

But it wasn't time to give up yet. We returned to Jozani to set up trail cameras, all the while playing leopard growls to see how the red colobus monkeys would react. Sure enough, the monkeys in the trees disappeared whenever I played the recording. Now, the sound of a leopard growling was pretty intimidating, so, even on a first listen, a monkey could decide to vacate the premises. But it was still a good sign that the monkeys, which were accustomed to stealing fruit from your plate, were at least alert enough to react with such alarm. It was the first indication that maybe a leopard had been there within the span of those monkeys' lifetimes. Yet, as far as evidence goes, it wasn't much.

Late that evening of that same day, I was taking a break with Patrick, beers in hand. I was pacing back and forth, thinking on my feet.

"I don't know what to do, man. We're coming to the end of the show. We really haven't found anything that's totally concrete. Sure, we're getting our message out, but I really hoped we would have found something, a really hard clue."

Patrick said, "What would you do if your life was on the line and you had to find out if there was a leopard in this jungle or not tomorrow?"

"I'd pull out all the stops."

"Well, what does that mean?"

"What does your cat love at home?"

"Oh, it loves little dangly treats."

"Well, that's the key."

"What is?"

"Tomorrow, we're going to the meat market in Stone Town. We're going to buy 150 pounds of meat and we're going to go back to the jungle and hang this meat from a tree. We're going to find a perfect tree that looks like a kitty cat's play den, and we're going to hang all these dangly, nasty bits of rotting meat from it."

This wasn't the first time Patrick and I had plotted our future over drinks. It had worked when we came up with the idea for *Hunting Lazarus*, and it worked then when we conceived of a strategy that was essentially recreating a Petco display in a jungle on the bottom of the world. But the science was sound. The scent of the meat would be up off the ground and would permeate farther into the surrounding jungle. And the spinning bits of flesh would trigger any feline to investigate. Up until that point, we had deployed my usual bag of technological tricks: thermal drones, night vision, audio recordings, HECS® gear, and trail cameras. But with help from late-night inspiration, we devised a hybrid strategy that combined modern gadgetry with basic instinct.

The next day we went to the market in Stone Town, which happens to be one of the liveliest places I had ever been. Food carts filled the streets. The surf of the Indian Ocean crashed near the base of an old stone fort that had been turned into a labyrinth of shops and that, at night, was strung with glittering lights. It was ironic that I'd be solving a leopard problem with a trip downtown, but I bought all the meat we could carry and returned to the park to festoon a tree in the jungle, which we renamed "the meat tree." It looked a little bit like we were on the set of *Texas Chainsaw Massacre* (the original), but if there was a leopard in the area, it was going to love it. We set camera traps around and along game trails leading to the area and then left to let the meat tree work its magic. You never know what you're going to find on trail camera footage. Just a week earlier we had recorded high-definition footage of a servaline genet in Zanzibar; it was groundbreaking scientific stuff to have high-definition video of this animal that no one had ever filmed before. (Norwegian scientists in 2003 had successfully captured still photographs of the servaline genet in Zanzibar, but ours was the first live footage.) Now Mitchell had tried to make it a rule that I would never look at the trail cameras without him. He wanted to catch the moment of discovery. But on an average expedition, we'll have used thirty trail cameras, and each one has approximately 2,000 clips on them. So, for Mitch to sit there and film me while I went through 2,000 clips on one of thirty trail cameras, he might as well have been back with me in the Channel Islands, filming as I counted ants. Even when you have a film crew following you around, the scientific method doesn't change. It comes down to grinding. It comes down to the monotony of sifting through data.

A week later, after we had collected the trail cameras, I decided to get a head start on reviewing the footage as we drove from the park to the hotel for a full night's rest. Sitting in the back of the bus, I opened my laptop and plugged in a memory card from one of the cameras. I went through thirty clips and saw a squirrel. I went through thirty more and nothing. About halfway through the three-hour ride to the hotel, I had already scanned hundreds of clips and then popped in another card. There was only one clip on the card and it lacked the false tapings, like tree branches blowing in the wind, that most often trigger the camera. And the one clip showed me something that I never thought I'd see and that the world hadn't seen in two decades: an adult leopard padding upon the jungle floor, moving from left to right through the camera frame, and disappearing between two giant trees. I watched it again. And again. I looked at my hands, which were shaking, and touched my face to make sure I wasn't dreaming. I watched it twenty times before saying anything to the crew. I had to push past the unreality of the moment. And when I couldn't hold back the excitement any longer, I screamed, "Pull over! Pull over! Pull the bus over!" We swerved to the side of the road. Everyone probably thought I had another taipan wrapped around my feet. I showed them the video. Mitch flipped on the camera he had on his lap. (He was, and is to this day, furious with me for even looking at the camera cards without him, because he wanted to be filming in the bush where I was supposed to have done it, rather than in the back of a dark bus without him even rolling.) Mitch captured everything from my screaming onward, including when I stood up and head-butted our sound guy. I didn't know I was going to do that, and he didn't see it coming. I was not in control of myself. I was having an out-of-body experience because right there, for everyone to see, was this incredible, astounding footage that changed our understanding of wildlife science. It upended the definitive factors cited by the IUCN when the organization declared the Zanzibar leopard extinct. And it was right here in my lap. David had beaten Goliath. The impossible had just become possible, and it dawned on me, right when I was looking at my shaking hands, that our work had huge ramifications for global conservation.

I realized that *Extinct or Alive* was not just about telling a story about what remains to be saved, though that will always be an important piece of the show's message. But we had done the big thing, we had delivered on what had been a quixotic hope and brought an animal back to life. With two or three seconds of footage from a trail camera, we had rewritten natural history as we knew it. We had flipped the notion of extinction on its head and upended the idea that human beings know everything when it comes to wildlife.

But hand in hand with the hopefulness created by our discovery, I need to make an important point: extinction is serious. The IUCN and other conservation organizations do vital work and do it exceptionally well. The term "extinction" is not overblown. Most often, it describes a tragic, irreversible loss of life. I don't want someone to watch my show, hear that rhinos are going extinct, and then dismiss the claim as alarmist. That is not the case. Scientists who study critically endangered animals are very good at their jobs. Their work should not be ignored because, suddenly, we think extinction is a matter of perspective. And that's the fine line I have always struggled to walk on this show. I *do* want to challenge the notion that extinction is final when declared so by man. But I also *don't* want to downplay the severe threat of extinction. It is very real.

I respect, and *Extinct or Alive* will always respectfully portray, the scientists who, after years of careful work, declare that a certain species has reached a taxonomical dead end. Simultaneously, the show exists to question the labels we have created to describe a species' status—labels such as "least concern," "vulnerable," "endangered," "critically endangered," and "extinct." Of those labels, only "extinct" communicates utter finality. It is the most definite of them all. The animal is not hiding in some out-of-the-way spot. Extinction means it no longer occurs in the universe.

Rewriting Natural History (the First Time)

To watch the Zanzibar leopard stride back into the light of our knowing was profound. It transformed our work from entertainment to something of concrete good. Conservation efforts could now go into practice to try to save this animal and its habitat. The animal could become a poster child for those efforts. Maybe the government would enlarge the park or enforce stricter regulations. The discovery would provide the fuel to drive good work. In the case of Zanzibar, unfortunately, not much has changed since the show aired. But that is an exception compared to other countries where major legislative changes occurred as a result of our findings. I will share some of those stories later in the book.

If I'd had any doubt about whether I was the right person for this job, that went out the window with the discovery of the Zanzibar leopard. There will always be a shred of doubt about whether I can physically put my hands on the animal I am after. After all, if you told me to find a snake in my garden right now, even though there are probably a dozen of them, I probably couldn't. But because every now and then someone made a mistake when crossing a species name from the list of the living, and because of my serendipitous combination of skills and experiences, I knew I was doing work that was meant especially for me.

6

FACE THE BEAST

FACE THE BEAST

The discovery in Zanzibar created a lot of momentum. I was starting to gain a reputation in the international conservation community, and people were starting to take what we do very seriously. A television producer I spoke with at the time told me that we were no longer *Chasing Bigfoot* or *Expedition Mungo* or *The Curse of Oak Island*, all reasonably successful shows, but all purely entertainment. We were now our own thing. The fact that we were being compared to those shows to begin with only goes to show how crazy our goal was for *Extinct or Alive*. If you're looking for an extinct animal, you might as well go looking for the Loch Ness Monster, too. There was no point, because neither existed. But we proved that kind of thinking wrong and were now ready to run with our success.

STILL ALIVE

Having just completed eight expeditions back-to-back, I thought I was ready for anything. And so, Patrick, Eric, and I dreamed up another show called *Face the Beast*. The premise was that throughout history there have been notable mass murders of human beings by animals. Of course, we all know this is not what animals do. Animals don't just wake up one day and decide to kill a bunch of people. Animals want nothing to do with people. Why, then, have these mass attacks taken place? Why, in 1945, during the Battle of Ramree in Burma (now Myanmar), when the Allied forces were fighting to wrest control of an island from the Japanese, were 1,000 Japanese soldiers devoured by saltwater crocodiles in the span of two horrific days? It was an absolute wildlife mystery. There was no better term for it. Our idea was to retrace the footsteps of the Japanese soldiers, while offering fair play to both human and animal perspectives, demonizing neither, to see if we could come up with a viable theory.

Patrick, Eric, and I pitched the idea to the History channel's president of development in his office. Patrick and Eric were dressed in smart suits and totally in their element, whereas I had on my best button-down, breathable, outdoor shirt. They were floating answers to questions about how exactly we were going to accomplish what we were proposing. And what we were proposing was to capture and take genetic material from saltwater crocodiles that were possibly alive when the massacre took place, all in the deepest jungles of Southeast Asia, all while filming a television show. Because they are television producers and not wildlife biologists, they were getting some of the science and strategy wrong. So, I butted in to the conversation (totally not like me, I know) to answer the question I am most often asked before filming something new: "Can you really do this?" And that's what the development executive wanted to know, along with a bunch of other questions like, "Well, what if you can't get near the crocodile? What if the crocodiles are too dangerous? What if it's too scary?" His skepticism was justified. But we had just discovered an extinct species, and that goes a long way toward getting people to believe in you. It also helped that, a few years earlier, my friend Mark Romanov and I had created a fifteen-minute documentary on a shoestring budget in which we traveled to Banco Chinchorro on the border of Belize and Mexico and swam with crocodiles, American crocodiles, in salt water without cages to show that they weren't just deadly killing machines. I pulled up the film on my iPhone, fast-forwarded to the part where I was face-to-face with twelve-foot-long crocodiles, and said, "This is what I can do. Trust me when I tell you we can work with these crocodiles." The executive was suitably impressed, and we had ourselves a show on History.

What the executive didn't know was that this would be my first time working as executive producer and showrunner. Though I had never *officially* served in those roles for season one of *Extinct or Alive*, there was one expedition when circumstances forced me into the jobs. Because it is so indicative of what we face making television in treacherous places, I think the story serves as a fair preface for the challenges we would come to face in Myanmar.

One of the running jokes among crew members of *Extinct or Alive* was keeping count of how many times you got sick or ran to the bathroom. Gross, I know. But our bodies were constantly battered by unfamiliar bugs, viruses, and bacteria. Keeping score was a way to lighten our suffering. In Madagascar, one of the producers, a woman named Kendyl, who, at the time, was Patrick's girlfriend, came down with a fever. It was the same old story. She would fight it off for the remainder of the shoot like everyone else. But, four or five days later, her condition suddenly deteriorated. She had been complaining of a strange bite on her backside. It was in an area she didn't really want to share with a coworker, but she knew I was a trained medic and allowed me to inspect the problem. Right on the inside of her butt cheek, where she thought she had sat on a spider or had been bitten by a mosquito, was a completely septic bite, red and swollen tight, with a dark center. Earlier in the week, the local medic on the shoot had lanced the bite, which probably had made it worse by introducing bacteria into the wound. Now she was suffering from a staph infection as well as African tick-bite fever, and the combination of the two were literally killing her. She had to be evacuated from our shoot location to Johannesburg, from Johannesburg to New York City, and into the emergency room. It took eight or nine days before she was in the clear.

But when Kendyl left, so did Patrick. Before taking off with her, he took me aside.

"Look, Forrest, we've done seven of these together when I've been there. You know what I do, you've seen it, and I know you are a quick learner. If you want to come home right now and throw in the towel, then Animal Planet will understand. Or do you want to do this thing?"

"You mean, without you and without Kendyl, so no producer, just me and the crew?"

"Exactly."

"I got it."

So, they took off. They stayed in touch via satellite phone, updating us on Kendyl's condition. And I did exactly what I wanted to do on the shoot, which was to tell the story of the kisuala, a believed-to-be-extinct lemur. And if we didn't find it, we would shift the spotlight to the red ruffed lemur, which most certainly still existed and most certainly was critically endangered. The show turned out well. It rated highest of the season behind the Zanzibar leopard. And the producer-less production created this confidence-building revelation that I no longer needed the same direction and hand holding. It was a giant win for Patrick, too, who realized that he would no longer have to travel to remote backwaters on the other side of the world. We may have neglected to tell Animal Planet that Patrick wouldn't be on location for most of season two of *Extinct or Alive*. After all, no television executive would knowingly have their host as the executive producer and the show-runner at the same time.

I was riding this confidence into the production of History channel's *Face the Beast*. But the responsibilities would be more traditionally shared. And because History was a direct competitor of Discovery and Animal Planet, I couldn't appear on camera. I was going to be the executive producer and show-runner, rather than the talent. And this was when I learned that a lot of talent is "plug and play." You cast for someone with the right look and suitable skills, and they expect to be told exactly what to do: where to stand, what to say, where to walk. Whereas I had expected the two hosts we hired to come to the table with thorough research, ideas, applications for technology, and all the sorts of things that I had done for *Extinct or Alive*. But that was not the case. Great guys, though.

In preparation for the expedition, I turned once again to my friend Mark Romanov. He had more to his résumé than just a small-budget documentary with me. He worked for the BBC with David Attenborough. He had filmed for *Blue Planet*. He had filmed for *Planet Earth*. He was a world-class cameraman at the age of twenty-seven. When we made our documentary about American crocodiles, which we had titled *Dancing with Dragons*, we agreed that whatever came of the film we would split fifty-fifty. When I pulled up the video on my iPhone in the History offices, Mark officially became involved. I called him up right away to tell him I had sold a show based on our documentary.

"Where are we going?" he asked. "Back to Mexico with that nice clear water in that cushy resort?"

"Well," I said, "not exactly."

I hired Mark as a scout to travel ahead of the crew to remote Ramree Island, a place where no Westerner had been since World War II. I asked him to jump on a plane to Myanmar the next week to see if it was humanly possible to get to

Ramree to film the show. He said, "No problem." After finding a way, he arrived on the island, where every single child in the village came running out to touch his skin and hair because they had never seen a white person before. They had never seen a television with a white person, nothing. This was first contact and as remote as it gets in Southeast Asia. When Mark returned, I asked him what it was like.

He said, "Man, this is going to be tough. There's nowhere to stay. The locals have never seen white people before. The fixer doesn't speak a word of English. And there are no crocodiles." I didn't like the sound of that last part.

"I was there for two weeks, and in two weeks, I barely saw a crocodile," he continued, "I got a couple of glimpses in the distance, but they have been hunted to near extinction."

I passed the report along to Eric and Patrick, who didn't seem too concerned and responded by telling me about the crew they had hired for the project. Patrick was listing names and providing quick bios of each person.

"Alright, here's your cameraman. He's worked on *Spiderman* and *Mission Impossible*. Here's your sound guy. He recorded for Blink-182. And here's . . . "

I interrupted him and told him I didn't think so. I wasn't using his guys. He didn't love the sound of that.

"Are you travelling to Myanmar?" I asked.

He told me Myanmar was out of his comfort zone and gamely inquired as to whom I was planning to use. I told him that Mark Romanov would serve as director of photography, Mitch Long from *Extinct or Alive* would continue working with me as a cameraman, and the rest were new guys who were my guys.

"Excuse me," Patrick said. "You're using new guys on a million-dollar project that we sold to History? Well, how much production experience do they have?"

I told him straight out that they had none. I was bringing on a sound guy from Australia, Trevor Robertson, who had worked in construction for fifteen years, could build anything, could fix anything, and just happened to know how to record sound and be damn good at it; and an assistant cameraman, John Harrington, who was my best dive buddy and the hardest-working guy I knew. Patrick was not okay with this. We were at an impasse. But eventually and reluctantly he agreed to use my crew on the condition that he send a producer of his choosing, which was how Ringo, which is not his real name, joined the team to make an already difficult job that much harder. In fact, the next few weeks in Myanmar were to be the most treacherous and unpredictable I had ever experienced in my television career.

We landed in Yangon, Myanmar. Our ragtag team was all together: Mark, Mitch, Trevor, John, Ringo, Eddie (our badass medic who came in very handy), and me. John looked green around the gills from having to oversee a half-million-dollars-worth of camera equipment. And Ringo, in his torn skinny jeans, moon boots, ultra-tight T-shirt, and neckerchief, looked like a cultural attaché from downtown Los Angeles. Still in the airport, we were joined by Somo, our fixer, who met us even before we had gone through customs. Security in Myanmar doesn't work the way it does elsewhere in the world, and Somo marched right up to us after we exited the plane.

"Hello, Mr. Forrest. Hello, Mr. Mark," said Somo by way of greeting, "Do you have drone?"

I told him that of course we had drones. We had three drones. And Somo knew we were bringing them. But the situation had changed, he told us. Three days earlier, a man had been arrested for using a drone to film what would come to be known as the Rohingya massacres. The man had been sentenced to life in prison. The government had just passed the new law. And we had $80,000 in drone equipment sitting in our cases. There were two possible courses of action. One option was to turn the drones over to the government and who knows if we would ever see them again. The second option, which is what we decided to do, was to sneak the equipment into the country. I made the executive decision and turned to Mitch.

"Build a wall out of our bags. Behind that wall, get the drones out of the cases, break them down, and split them up among our bags."

Mitch got to work and divvied up the drones between our carry-ons. We thought we were so clever. Thirty minutes later, we walked out of customs. Border officials had looked in our cases. No drones, no problem. Keep in mind that we had just learned that the punishment for having a drone in Myanmar was life in prison. It wasn't a slap on the wrist. It wasn't a fine. It was life in prison in a country where life in prison meant death. We walked away from the airport with our chests puffed

out, smiling and high-fiving, because with a bit of quick thinking we had cruised into the country.

We jumped into a van and off we went toward Ramree
Island. This was no easy trip. Once we got out of Yangon, it
was a twelve-hour drive, followed by a six-hour boat ride on
a long-tail boat to a tiny "research station." It was incredible
to see the impact of humanity melt away over the duration
of our travel. When we first embarked on the boat, the banks
of the river were covered in garbage—plastic and tires. But
the farther we rode, the wilder and wilder it became, until
floating plastic bottles were replaced by floating mangroves,
and the smell of burning tires was replaced by the smell of
dense, salty, ocean air. The transition was indicative of what it
means to get away from human beings. The research station
was rustic, to put it mildly. I had never seen one this bad. Even
though it had been constructed within the previous few years,
it was struggling to hold itself together. The mangrove swamp
was quickly reclaiming it. Mud soaked the walls and pushed
up from between the floorboards. The bugs were outrageous.
This being an open-air structure, they had free rein. So did the
bats. One bat flew up from under Mitch's bed, trapping itself
in his mosquito netting and causing Mitch to shout for help
until we could work a release. There were little mud skippers,
fish that emerge from the tidal flat to joust with each other
on top of the mud, all around the station. There were eagles
overhead and fishing in the river. The station was literally surrounded, almost as if it were being digested by the estuarine
environment. We were in the middle of a mangrove swamp, the

only habitat that upright, bipedal, terrestrial organisms, namely humans, could not physically move through. You sink into the mud with every step, and the vegetation is nearly impassable. I couldn't help but think of all the Japanese soldiers fighting their way through this muck. Trying to shoot a television show was not going to be easy.

There I was at twenty-nine years old, responsible for a million-dollar show with a crew of six guys, two of whom had never worked in television before. I had a kooky producer who was out of step with the environment and how I worked. We had traveled to a part of Myanmar that hadn't seen Westerners for decades, and our job was to trace the path of Japanese soldiers from World War II and then determine what led to their mass murder by crocodiles, all while staying alive ourselves and making some decent television. It was a lot to take on.

I didn't have a lot of time to worry about it. On the first day, we learned that a notorious crocodile had been spotted in the area. The animal had a big, white scar on his face. Our host, Andrew Ucles, who is a crocodilian expert in his own right, theorized that the scar was from a soldier's bayonet, which it very well could have been. The crocodile was eighteen to twenty feet long. It was immense and could have been alive, eating people, during World War II.

We met with a villager whose wife had been killed three weeks earlier by this crocodile. The man showed us pictures of how she had been ripped apart and drowned. He described the horror of the day. It was a sad and heavy moment on that beautiful, remote swamp in the middle of Southeast Asia. His loss reinforced the danger of what we were there to do.

For days we trekked neck-deep through mud, destroying much of our equipment as we fought the elements to retrace the steps of the Japanese soldiers. In our slow progress, we found a human skull—not a prop, not something for television—a cranium buried in the mud around a small ruin. We found an old, World War II military-issued rifle. We found the remains of the Japanese's semipermanent encampment. The trail had not run cold. We spoke with elder locals and eventually developed a compelling theory for what happened there in 1945. Ramree Island was an extremely isolated outpost for an encampment of soldiers. Getting supplies like fresh food to them would have been terribly difficult if not impossible. The likelihood that the soldiers hunted and ate every edible morsel on the island was high. So, as the soldiers emptied the forests of wildlife, the sizable population of saltwater crocodiles starved. When certain animals face a prolonged period of scarcity, they can enter a state known as "torpor," wherein their metabolic functions slow in order to conserve energy. And when food becomes available, an animal can snap out of torpor right away. Our theory then was that there were hundreds of starving crocodiles outside the military camp. As the British fought to retake the island, the Japanese soldiers were pushed into the swamp, and several hundred crocodiles snapped out of torpor at once and experienced something that biologists call "henhouse syndrome." Imagine a fox getting into a chicken coop. It is so overwhelmed with the amount of prey that it just kills every chicken in the coop because it can. Not because it needs to, not because it is starving even, but because its predator instinct overtakes its rational brain and makes it kill everything in its power.

If true, and the evidence thus far supports our theory, then this was a revelation. We had all worked together (except for a certain producer) and were elated to have figured this out. We were two days from departing and had the show in the bag. Nothing terrible had happened, even though we had lots of cuts, scrapes, and bruises. We had even seen crocodiles. We had found them and spotted White Nose, the one responsible for killing a woman only a few weeks earlier. Then, at the crack of dawn the next day, we heard brutal screams.

The research station was situated directly across from a small fishing village, with a broad, placid expanse of water in between. Only about eight people live in the village, and one of them was screaming.

"Get up, get up, get up, something's going on," I shouted and roused the crew.

We jumped into the speedboat, the one we had chartered to get us to the station in nine hours, and rode up to the village. We saw a boy, about fifteen years old, limp, being dragged up to one of the huts nearest the water. White Nose had struck again. The boy was bleeding to death. His arm was broken in a dozen or more places. Profound trauma such as this occurs when a crocodile bites a limb and then goes into a "death roll," spinning its body in the water, in order to rip the body part away. The croc hadn't managed to rip this boy's arm off, but it looked like it had been through a woodchipper. The boy also had a huge gash on the inside of his thigh, near his groin, right next to his femoral artery. Fortunately, I am medically trained, and we had another medic with us, Eddie, and we went to work. Our two hosts were rooted to the spot since coming upon the scene. So, I started screaming orders.

"Andrew, go and get that hammock. Cut it off the tree."

He ran over and started cutting off the hammock. Meanwhile, I was elbow deep in blood, trying to stop this kid from bleeding out. I shouted to the other host, Brian.

"Go and cut down those two poles. Make a stretcher."

Andrew and Brian were weaving together a stretcher from the hammock and two bamboo poles, using zip ties to secure it. The kid's mother was wailing and had already given him up for lost. She told us he was dead, insisted he was gone. But he was still conscious and by some miracle we managed to stop the bleeding. We didn't make any stitches. We just did compression bandages all over him. Fortunately, the femoral artery, which was so close to the big gash on the inside of his thigh, was not severed. We taped his two legs together because if he were dropped or if he kicked his leg out or anything like that, that cut could have spread another half an inch and that would have been it. Still, his mother had abandoned all hope. She knew there was no hospital access for them. There was no medicine. There was no running water. Even if her son somehow pulled out of his accident, he would have gone septic and died. There was no question about that. But fate shined in this instance because there was the speedboat.

Face the Beast

We carefully secured the boy on the stretcher into the boat and told the driver to, "Go, go, go." The driver rushed him to the nearest hospital six hours away, and the boy lived. His arm was removed—or that's what we heard from our fixer, though we've never had confirmation on that. He returned to his village less than a month later. We took care of his medical bills and other expenses, and we were just so grateful that we were there with everything we needed to save this boy's life.

But the story didn't end there. The mood among the crew had gotten heavy. We had all been fighting with Ringo. We had been worn down by unpleasantness. Then, to add insult to injury, Somo, our fixer, got a call. How they managed to reach him on our satellite phone, I'll never know. He picked up the receiver and was quickly in a heated conversation, shouting in Burmese. But the longer the conversation continued, the quieter he became. His face fell into a deep frown as he listened. Normally, Somo was a happy and bubbly person, but something was wrong. He hung up the phone and slumped his head.

"Somo, what's going on?" I asked him.

He raised his eyes to me with tears running down his cheeks. I assumed the worst. The boy had died. His wounds were too severe, or he hadn't arrived at the hospital in time. But that wasn't it at all. The call had come from customs. CCTV security cameras had, clear as day, filmed us pulling out our drones, breaking them down, and putting them in our various backpacks and then smuggling them out of the airport.

Somo had just been told that on our return to Yangon, we were to proceed straight to the airport and turn ourselves, and the drones, over to the authorities, and that we were going to jail. As you can imagine, this was troublesome news. A death sentence was being handed down to all of us, and ours wasn't going to be fixed by some timely first aid. I called my line producer and told him the situation.

"There's nothing we can do," he said. "We can't go to the US consulate with that. You guys broke the law."

"Well," I said, "fuck you, man."

I sat down with my crew and broke the news to them. Suddenly, I was looking at the faces of very unhappy people. John Harrington was twenty-two years old, my best spearfishing buddy, and this was his first production. He had saved a kid's life. He had been neck-deep in mud for weeks. And now he was told he's going to jail in Myanmar. I don't think he thought that was how TV worked.

"What are we going to do?" John asked.

"Have we got all our drone shots?"

"We sure do."

"Okay. Pull the cards, back up all the footage, put those hard drives somewhere deep in a case, and throw those drones in the river."

"Don't give them to Somo?"

"Nope, don't give them to Somo. I don't know what they'll do to Somo. I don't know what they'll do at all. But you take those drones, and you throw them in the swamp."

"Okay."

The guys pulled the cards, backed up the footage, and, sure enough, we had an unceremonious tossing of drones right into the swamp, probably the only time I've ever polluted in my life. There they sank, $80,000 in flying cameras.

We still had two days on the shoot. We've just watched a kid get mauled. We've just been told we're going to jail for life in Myanmar. So, I looked to the guys.

"We've come this far. You guys want to throw in the towel? Or do you want to try and finish this thing?"

Ringo, of course, our producer, was the first to respond.

"We're out of here. I hate this and I hate you guys."

But my crew came through.

"We're in this to do it right. Let's finish it up. Let's go. We've got two days to catch this croc."

On the last night, Andrew Ucles and I built a trap, basically using Andrew as bait. And guess who showed up for dinner? Mister White Nose himself. Andrew got a noose around White Nose's neck, wrangled, and subdued the eighteen-foot, one-hundred-year-old dinosaur that had likely killed dozens of people over the years. With the croc under our power, killing or relocating the animal seemed reasonable under the circumstances. There had been two attacks in the previous three weeks, both of which would have surely been fatal if we hadn't been nearby to save the boy. But the animal's fate was not ours to decide. We brought the case to the village elders. Five elders from different villages throughout the swamp convened to determine what would be done with the crocodile known as White Nose.

"What do you guys want to do?" I asked one of the elders.

"Let him go."

"What?"

"We live in *his* swamp. We are his guests here. These things happen in Myanmar. Let the crocodile go."

It was one of the most impactful conversations I have ever had. As in Africa, here was a group of people who understood their place in the food chain. It wasn't that they wanted other people to die. It wasn't that they wanted the crocodile to hurt anybody. But they understood that their crocodiles were few and far between and that this swamp had always been its home. It deserved to be there.

We took a tissue sample, took some DNA from him, measured him, and then let him go. That was the end of the shoot. We called it a wrap and then had to head back to Yangon. The business with the crocodile had distracted us, but the heaviness of uncertainty settled back on our chests. We had to find a way out of Myanmar. During those final two days of the shoot, however, I had placed a call to an acquaintance of mine, an individual with something of a checkered past. He was an ex-mercenary who lived in New Zealand. It doesn't matter how I know him, but he was just the kind of person whose help we could use.

"Hey, we've got $1 million worth of footage sitting on hard drives and we might be going to jail," I told him. "Will you fly into Yangon, pick up some hard drives, and then fly out?"

He said, "Sure will."

Soon after, he sent me instructions for the exchange, telling me he would be waiting at a specific intersection.

"I will be in a black SUV. I will pull up to the stoplight next to you. You roll down your window, I roll down my window, and you hand the drives through the window. We will exchange no words. And I will not tell anybody."

It was a plan. We returned to Yangon and checked into a different hotel than the one we had stayed in when we arrived. I drove to the intersection where my acquaintance had told me to meet him, pulling up at the stoplight. A black SUV appeared next to the driver-side window. I recognized the man inside wearing dark sunglasses. Our windows went down. A paper bag went from one vehicle to the other. The windows rolled up, and that was the last time I ever saw those hard drives. They were off. I received confirmation through a cryptic text message that the eagle had landed, so to speak. Wending their way through the southern hemisphere, the footage eventually made its way back to the States and allowed me to fulfill my contractual obligations to the History channel.

The footage had gotten out of the country and now it was our turn. We were hunkered down in our hotel. We hadn't turned ourselves in. I sat down with my crew and Somo.

"Look, they're looking for us. We know they want us to turn ourselves in. The footage is gone. They have no proof of anything other than whatever CCTV proof they have. The drones are gone. They're sitting at the bottom of a swamp 600 miles from here. We've got two options. We can either load up in some vans, make a break for the Thai border, cross into Thailand, and then fly out from there. But if we're caught doing that, it's obvious that we're doing something wrong. The other option is to get in the cars tomorrow, show up in three separate groups to the airport, check in individually rather than as a group, and see what happens. Keep in mind, this is a country where you can just walk through customs and nobody pays attention. What do you guys think?"

Everyone made a lot of indecisive noises, and then we had a vote. By one vote, we decided to fly back on our original flights, arriving in groups, hoping for the best. We arrived at the airport the next day and waited in line to check in. Unlike in Ramree Island, white people come in and out of Yangon all the time, so we weren't sticking out like sore thumbs. As we neared the security desk, we realized that the airline's computer system was down, and passengers were checking in by signing their names on a piece of paper. This was probably a regular occurrence at the airport in Yangon, but the timing was exquisite. We signed our names and checked three or four bags each. We stayed separate and didn't make eye contact with anyone in any of the other groups. We proceeded toward our gate, boarded the plane as quickly as we could, and struggled to maintain composure as we slipped past security for a second time. Once we had achieved cruising altitude, we let the cheers rip. But as soon as we landed, I found out that an airport employee had lost his job because he had failed to stop us and that Somo, our fixer, had been arrested. He went to jail and was held overnight. But because they had no footage of

My grandfather and I fishing on the banks of the Zambezi River in Mana Pools, as a big bull elephant comes down to take a drink. *Jacaranda Summerfield*

Snuggling up with Fara, the serval kitten, who we found while tiling a field on the farm in Zimbabwe. *Jacaranda Summerfield*

On safari as a youngster. Even then, I thought if I wore clothes that looked like the animals, I could get closer to them. *Jacaranda Summerfield*

My first big tiger fish pulled out of the Zambezi River, the proudest I have ever been to catch a fish! *Jacaranda Summerfield*

Volunteering at the crocodile farm on Benguerra Island, Mozambique. It's here that my intense fascination with crocodilians began. *Jacaranda Summerfield*

My sister and I on Christmas morning with all of our best friends, the farm workers' children. We were lining up to receive presents, and, as you will surely notice, it's ladies first on the right-hand side! *Jacaranda Summerfield*

Capturing my first giant anaconda on spring break in the Amazon the morning of my twenty-first birthday. March 31, 2009. *Mike Knoerr*

"Albert Girther," a ginormous lobster that I caught and named that made international headlines when I couldn't bring myself to kill it. He lived in an aquarium for a few weeks, before being returned to a marine sanctuary to live out his days. *Adam Schewitz*

Running toward a water source (for a much-needed skinny dip) in the Namibian Desert. Sand EVERYWHERE. *Jessica Summerfield*

Diving in the famous Jellyfish Lake, Palau, before the population crash. Swimming here felt like swimming in a giant cup of *boba* tea! *Jessica Summerfield*

Fulfilling a lifelong dream of meeting a Komodo dragon, on Komodo island, Indonesia. Notice the coral burn on my right bicep from hunting for lobster to feed ourselves. That scar reminds me every day of these amazing dragons. *Jessica Summerfield*

Spearfishing for the prized white sea bass in Southern California. *Kevin Glen*

Filming *Extinct or Alive: The Tasmanian Tiger* for Animal Planet's Monster week, January 2016. I was more interested in the trail camera footage on my laptop than I was in the cameras pointed in my face. *Chris Darnell*

Observing a juvenile cassowary (while keeping a sharp eye out for its mother, who we soon encountered) in the jungles of Far North Queensland, Australia, during season one of *Extinct or Alive*. *James Brantley*

Repelling down a terrifying 1,200-foot cliff to look for nesting sea birds in the Faroe Islands. In my hands is a stunning puffin, a sea bird that I have always wanted to see in person. *Mitchell Long*

A combination of high tech and traditional camo: HECS™ technology mixed with leaves of the Javanese jungle to create a ghillie suit for a long night of predator calling to attempt to film a presumably extinct Javan tiger. *Mitchell Long*

Mitchell, Neil, Chris, and I posing in front of the infamous "meat tree." This picture was snapped about four hours before the most earth-shattering discovery of my life to that point, the Zanzibar leopard. *Patrick DeLuca*

Freediving with an incredible tiger shark in the Bahamas while attempting to secure a fecal sample to test for trace evidence of Caribbean monk seals. *Mark Romanov*

My beautiful wife, Jessica, poses with a bull shark and holds up the tail of a specimen of a presumed extinct Pondicherry shark, moments after trading a box of cigarettes for it, in a fishing village in Sri Lanka. *Donald Schultz*

Two local villagers in Myanmar who were identifying a crocodile known as "white nose" during the History Channel shoot for *Face the Beast*. *Trevor Robertson*

Attempting to locate extinct shark species means fishing in very unlikely spots, including spots that herds of water buffalo like to wallow in. Sri Lanka, November 2018. *Mark Romanov*

Gently pulling a fur sample from a rescued wolf that resembles the extinct subspecies of the southern Rocky Mountain wolf. *Mitchell Long*

Posing with an incredibly rare fossa, Madagascar's largest carnivore and a dream species for me to see in the wild. *Mitchell Long*

Johnny, me, Rob, and Mitchell geared up in ghillie suits to look like flotsam before drifting down a river in Vietnam to look for the legendary saola in the Annamite Mountains. *Mark Romanov*

Sitting patiently in the chaparral scrub of Southern California while watching the annual spring bird migration. *John Harrington*

Sunburnt and exhausted, I sit on the banks of the Rio Apaporis River in the heart of FARC rebel–controlled Colombian Amazon, holding in my hands the "lost" Rio Apaporis caiman I had just captured, which had not been seen by western science in nearly forty years. *John Harrington*

After discovering Fern (a tortoise species lost for 114 years), an impromptu tortoise stretcher was quickly constructed to safely relocate her to the Fausto Llerena Breeding Center on Isla Santa Cruz, Galápagos. *Mark Romanov*

Mitchell helps me hold the door as we set a giant customized crocodile trap that we fabricated overnight in Palu, Indonesia, in an attempt to capture the legendary "Tire Croc." *Opn Images*

Facing off with an American crocodile in the clear Mexican waters while trying to prove they are not mindless killing machines. I didn't even know there was a second croc in the background until reviewing the pictures later! *Mark Romanov*

Jessica and I untangle a saltwater crocodile from a seine net that we were using to survey a lagoon for shark species. *Donald Schultz*

I stand holding the truest icon of extinction, the pangolin that every day edges closer to its demise. This beautiful scaled mammal is a victim of its own uniqueness. *Mitchell Long*

Rushing to save the life of the crocodile attack victim in Myanmar. He lost the arm but kept his life due to our quick work and even quicker speedboat. *John Harrington*

Somo with the drones, only of the white Americans divvying up the hardware, he had to be released and nothing more came of it.

Still, I won't be going back to Myanmar anytime soon.

I have already described the weird lull between wrapping a shoot and airing an episode. It followed the filming of *Naked and Afraid* as well as the filming of the pilot episode for *Extinct or Alive*. You get on with your life. You forget about what you have done and what is coming. And, if you're lucky (and I had enjoyed my fair share of good fortune to this point), the show airs and your career, your mission, takes another step toward its ultimate destination, whatever that happens to be. What was different this time around was that I wasn't some contestant operating within the preestablished rules of a show, and I wasn't a host lending the on-camera personality to a giant operation taking place off camera. I was the producer, the person responsible for the budget, the crew, the footage, the result, the story . . . all of it, the whole mountain of logistics. So, whatever happened when the show aired wouldn't change that I was now making different waves in the world of television. Sure, I could find an animal that didn't want to be found, but now I was showing that I could make television where others dared not tread.

I would like to tell you that when *Face the Beast* came out, it was a massive success, that people loved it, and that my career skyrocketed ever upward to stardom, but that wasn't the case at all. After everything we had gone through—surviving the mud, solving a historical riddle, capturing an infamous crocodile, saving a boy's life, saving our own—the History channel didn't like the way we had structured the episode. They reorganized it again and again and then premiered our show at the tail end of a six-hour marathon of *Forged in Fire* (a show about making knives and swords) at 10:00 p.m. The ratings weren't good, and the show didn't continue. Our efforts hadn't led to the short-term outcome we had hoped for. (I'll always have a bone to pick with History for that 10:00 p.m. time slot.) But I was beginning to see that our experiences would earn out in the long term.

REALITY
CHECK

REALITY CHECK

Whether for *Extinct or Alive* or *Face the Beast*, I was encountering communities, the world over, where troubling losses of wildlife had occurred. In various locations, the pressures of hunting, development, and human ignorance all took a similar toll, decimating ecosystems that had supported top predators or other key species. But whether I was in Tasmania, Taiwan, or Myanmar, the people there understood the role they had played. There was a communal sense of remorse. They were aware of their mistakes, wanted to change, and were willing to work toward a solution. The television platform I was building allowed me to share those silver-lining stories of human awakening, of a light at the end of the tunnel. But if you are familiar with season one of *Extinct or Alive*, you'll know there was one episode that revealed how the forces of extinction continue to thrive within deeply embedded cultural mentalities.

Denmark's Faroe Islands are austere, mythic shards of rock that jut from the cold waters of the North Atlantic. They were once home to vast colonies of a black-and-white flightless seabird known as the great auk, a species that ranged from Newfoundland to the Iberian Peninsula. Their population soared into the hundreds of millions, wherein they would cover every available nook and crevice in the rock faces of the Faroes. They existed in much the same way that Antarctic penguins do today. Unfortunately, as we all know, industrialization started early in the North Atlantic and resulted in the destruction of ancient, natural systems. Auks were prized for their down feathers, which could be stuffed into pillows, comforters, and similar products. They were prized also for the ease of harvesting them. All a hunter had to do was row or walk up to one, bop it on the head, and throw it in the boat. Entire communities were built upon the business of harvesting auk feathers, and today the ruins of villages, communities that subsisted entirely on this trade, can be seen moldering along the shoreline. The great auk is thought to have gone extinct in 1850.

But, despite centuries of exploitation, the animal's historic range, which spanned an entire ocean, seemed large enough to offer some possibility that small populations had survived. Our research focused on the Faroes, which were at the center of this range. We assessed whether there was enough prey, whether there were landing areas where birds could emerge from the violent surf without smashing themselves to pieces on the unforgiving rocks, and whether there were sightings or other evidence that might lead us to their rediscovery. There was one rumor that eggs, potentially from a great auk, had been found only ten or fifteen years earlier. We were excited to travel there and to search for this lost bird. I even found myself preparing to rappel down a 1,200-foot cliff to inspect ledges and crevices for potential nesting sites. I don't like to advertise this, but I am maybe more than a little acrophobic. I do not like heights. I try to think of myself as brave when I fight through these fearful moments. I remember talking to Mitch over the walkie.

"I don't want to do this. I don't want to do this."

"You don't have to!" was his reassuring reply; but, of course, I did have to.

I closed my eyes, a terrible idea, as I took my first step backward off the cliff. I just didn't have it in me to keep my eyes open for that first step.

But eyes wide open or not, we found no signs of eggs or nests, except for those of puffins.

Sure, we sailed in a 200-year-old Viking sailboat, which was cool. We explored the remotest parts of the islands and clambered up cliff faces to catch puffins. It was an incredible journey, but I came away believing with every ounce of my being that the great auk no longer existed. Somehow, we had eradicated untold millions of these amazing birds until none were left. But this wasn't the saddest part of the story. The hope for the great auk was always a dim one, and as I've said, the chances of finding an extinct species in two weeks is an epic long shot. What wounded me to my soul, what took my breath away with its cruelty and madness, occurred at the very start of filming.

Now, of all places in the world, the Faroe Islands, a territory of the Kingdom of Denmark, a white, upper-class, first-world nation, might be expected to be at the forefront of conservation. After all, affluent and educated societies are the ones that can afford the luxury of conservation. If a population has food in its belly and a place to rest its head, so to speak, then the governing body can turn to less pressing matters such as environmental integrity. So, within this Northern European nation is a tradition called the grind. The grind is the slaughter of pilot whales that has been happening since the Faroe Islands were first settled 1,200 years ago. For hundreds of years, when a pod of pilot whales would swim near the islands, villagers would all jump in their wooden canoes, paddle alongside the moving pod of whales, and work to break off an individual away from its family, driving the whale into a bay, where they could surround the animal and slaughter it. The hunt could take days. So, for the amount of effort, skill, and risk that went into pursuing and killing that animal, you almost have to admire the accomplishment. And those hunters were spurred on by a worthy goal: to harvest an animal that would sustain the whole community. The meat would be butchered and dried and the blubber rendered into oil. The village depended on the resource of the whales, using every ounce of their kill, and hunting only what they needed.

Those determined settlers reaped the bounty of the North Atlantic and through their efforts enabled the colonization of the archipelago.

But the tradition of the hunt had mutated into something grotesque by the time I traveled to the islands in 2018. We had had a hell of a time getting there. We flew in a small plane, taking off from Copenhagen, and attempted to land twice. Because of a storm, the plane nearly skidded off the runway both times. The tires would touch down. The pilot wouldn't like the grip of the tarmac and would pull back up into the sky, bringing us back to Copenhagen to await another attempt in better weather. We succeeded on the third attempt and dragged our bags to the hotel in the lovely capital of Tórshavn, an impeccably quaint and well-to-do city. Seemingly the moment we dropped down our stuff, exhausted from the prolonged travel, a loud bell, the town bell, sounded through the streets. Suddenly people were pouring out of buildings, congregating near the beach. We were told by our fixer, who happened to be the brother of the chief of police, that a grind was taking place. I should point out that *Whale Wars*, a show dedicated to stopping the slaughter of whales, spent two years sitting around the Faroe Islands, hoping to capture a grind in progress. But the timing never worked out, and they were eventually driven away by local authorities. My crew and I had been on the island for about three hours. I started rallying the crew to set up cameras and follow me to the beach. I remember Mitch turning to me right then.

"Are you sure you want to do this? You don't have to. This has nothing to do with *Extinct or Alive*."

He was right. This wasn't why we had traveled there. We had planned to search for and tell the story of the great auk. But my decision was an easy one to make.

"Mitch, if we don't shine a light on this, who will? Are we going to bury our heads in the sand pretending that this isn't happening, then go on our merry way making a show about wildlife and conservation?"

Mitch looked like he had expected that answer. He shook his head and told me this was going to be tough. I knew it was. But never in my nightmares could I have imagined the scene we were about to witness.

We ordered a taxi and jumped in with our fixer riding in the front passenger seat. I told the driver we wanted to go to the grind.

"Well, how are you going to view this?" The fixer asked me, apparently concerned with how I might present the hunt on my show. "People from outside don't like this."

"It's going to be hard for me," I admitted.

"Why? Don't you eat chicken?"

"Of course I eat chicken."

"Well, what's the difference between a chicken and a whale?"

"For one, chickens are farmed. They are not endangered. In fact, they're overpopulated. For two, they're not intelligent beings at the top of the food chain like a whale."

The fixer paused, maybe to think on my points.

Reality Check

"Yeah, but it's just meat, just like a whale."

Maybe not. I realized right then and there before even witnessing the grind that if that was their mentality, that a whale was equal to a chicken, then the Faroese were willfully missing the point. I understand that acknowledging the difference between life-forms is an unpopular opinion among vegans and animal rights activists. But it is biological truth. For example, if you're an ant, and if you are one ant in a colony of hundreds of thousands, then you, the individual ant, are not as valuable to the ecosystem as a snow leopard. Activists would argue with me over this. But there are an estimated 4,000 to 6,000 snow leopards left in the wild. The fact is that a snow leopard is an apex predator, controlling prey populations and removing carrion. If you laid out ten dead ants next to ten dead snow leopards, could you tell the difference? Could you decide that one loss was greater than the other? Comparing a chicken to a whale was equally absurd and was an example of sloppy, impoverished, self-serving thinking.

The taxi pulled up to a gathering of hundreds of people. Everyone there was an islander. My impression was that to receive meat from the hunt, an islander needed to participate, so there was no shortage of attendees. I have since read that participants must also receive training in the use of a spinal-cord lance so as not to cause the animal undue suffering. What a joke. As you might expect, I'm not the first critic of the grind. Environmental groups have been attacking the practice since the 1980s. But the Faroese government continues to support the tradition, citing its historic roots, the small number of animals taken annually (a number, since the early 2000s, that ranges from a few hundred individuals to more than 1,000), and the necessity of the whales as a food source. In a city with flashy nightclubs and high-end sushi restaurants, where everyone drives new cars, social welfare supports citizens of one of the highest-performing economies in the world, and you can find just about any modern amenity you can think of, I find the "necessary food source" defense not only weak but deeply disingenuous.

So, with these several thousand people milling about, waiting for what came next, we popped out of the taxi with our cameras. Sure enough, the police came right over to shut us down. But our fixer must have been showing off (I believe it was the first time he'd ever fixed a television production) and told the officer to fetch the police chief. When he arrived, our fixer, who must have been the chief's older brother, insisted that we could film the event and that there was no reason to worry. We explained that we were there to film the grind and that I would give my opinion of the practice. We weren't there to sugarcoat it. We didn't lie or hide our intentions. Apparently, our fixer's insistence along with our honesty were enough to permit our filming, and we became one of the first groups of outsiders to ever document a grind.

We stood on the rocky beach, awaiting the start of this age-old hunt to begin. I don't know if I expected to see actual canoes in the water, but I didn't expect to see a literal armada of extravagantly expensive boats arriving on the outskirts of the bay. These were some of the nicest fishing boats that money can buy, costing at least $100,000 to maybe upwards of $1,000,000. These were not grungy fishing boats that you would see docked in Californian or New York harbors. These were luxury brands reserved for the Miami boat show.

"What's going on?" I asked my fixer.

"Those are the boats that are pushing the whales."

"I thought the grind was done with canoes."

"Oh, not for a hundred years. Why would we use canoes?"

I need to reiterate the absurdity of this, the self-indulgent barbarity of a wealthy nation conducting a supposedly traditional hunt with a fleet of gleaming yachts. I thought to myself, *I suppose efficiency would increase even in this.* Why waste a week of paddling when, with powerboats, you could break off a whale from the pod in an afternoon? But even this assumption quickly proved to be another miscalculation. The armada wasn't chasing a single whale, it was pushing an entire pod of eighty-eight pilot whales toward the shore. Mothers and their three-foot-long calves. Fathers, sons, sisters, daughters. A whole, precious, familial web. They were being herded toward certain death on the shore. This was only the second pod of pilot whales to pass the island that year. The first had been entirely destroyed. It seemed like every human inhabitant of this island territory was waiting on the beach.

Before I saw the whales, I heard them. Even over the roar of the engines, over the chaos of firecrackers used to scare the whales forward, over the people slapping the water, I heard the songs of the whales. In any other circumstance, such a sound would bring you to your knees with its beauty. But these were not songs of delight and joy. These were songs of terror. They were so loud, so penetrative and vibrant, you could hear them even while standing out of the water.

I watched as the whales drew closer and closer to the shore. Children, their parents, and grandparents were waiting with pitchforks, machetes, kitchen knives, screwdrivers, anything that could stab and kill and murder. It was as if a bloodthirsty trance had descended over this nation. I imagine that 200 years ago, hundreds if not thousands of pods would pass the island each year. Now, this was only the second, and it was to be destroyed, like the one that came before it, by these people with awful tools. The first pilot whale beached itself, and a crowd fell upon it in a mad frenzy, stabbing, kicking, jabbing, and bludgeoning this magnificent, harmless, beautiful creature, an animal that had never experienced such terror or fear. A calf then followed, just three feet long, no longer than my dog, washing up on the beach. I watched as a boy, maybe nine years old, stabbed the calf in the head with a screwdriver. The mother, trying to protect her calf, beached right alongside it and was stabbed in the face with a pitchfork. And so on. The sea turned red with blood. I do not say this proverbially. The bay was frothing with dying, screaming animals. Their blood sloshed around the legs of humans, who were baying themselves, until the last cry of the pod petered out.

It was just as I had described in Myanmar, what happens to starving crocodiles, this henhouse syndrome, where bloodlust and murderous rage overtook and transformed these people. I had never seen anything like it. Their affinity for taking life.

Their delight in the destruction of something so special and harmless. Of course, the major flaw of that comparison is that the crocodiles couldn't walk into town to a restaurant. They couldn't ask their onboard chef to prepare a meal for the guests staying on their yacht. They couldn't depend on the steady support of a government for their physical well-being. Those crocodiles were organisms on the brink of death, whereas the Faroese were killers for sport, for whatever twisted justification they mustered about their history as subsistence hunters and gatherers, which they were no longer. I watched them kill every animal in that pod.

I cried on the shore. I was unable to speak. If you asked my wife, she would tell you that I am not quick to tears. But I was broken. I couldn't move. I couldn't speak to the camera. My knees were weak. I had never been so rattled in my life. Not when I was chased out of my home by armed "war veterans" in Zimbabwe. Not when I was nearly paralyzed in Thailand. Not when I saw that boy mauled by a saltwater crocodile in Myanmar. I looked over at Mitch. His arms were shaking, and tears had washed his face. The footage was nearly unusable—at least not for television—because he was doing everything in his power to look through the lens to hold the shot, but he was breaking down in the same pain that I was. The difference between my crew's shock and grief and the elation of the islanders was stark, almost absurdly so, as if we were the chosen survivors of a slaughter.

This all occurred within our first few hours in the Faroe Islands, but the business of television prompted us back to the task at hand. We had the search for the great auk before us. But the sadness of the grind would infect the whole episode, and what we had just experienced didn't bode well for the possibility of the auk's continued existence. This was a nation built to consume its resources even to the point of consuming itself. Abandoned, crumbling structures that dotted the rocky islands testified to that fact. Those early settlements were built upon the killing of auks. When the auks were gone, what then happened to the people? This irresponsibility, this proud ignorance leading to self-destruction, is a microcosm of what the planet faces if we don't shift mentalities from murder to conservation. To think that in 2018, which is when I witnessed the grind, humans still had the mentality that they can endlessly take, leaving nothing behind, all while defending themselves with the thinly veiled lie of tradition, all while getting a sick thrill out of it, is disgusting and despicable. To this day, with everything that's ever happened in my life—and we've been through quite a lot already in this book—the grind was the most traumatic thing I have ever witnessed and is a perfect example of what can and will happen to us as a species and to all the living things on this planet if we continue to go unchecked.

We returned to the United States feeling beaten and broken. Yet we produced a raw and intense episode with an important message. We turned in the rough cut to Animal Planet, which included about five minutes of the killing of the pilot whales. Knowing what I do now, I should have expected the response we received from Animal Planet. They told me to take it out, to cut mention of the grind. I nearly flipped the desk in my office when I heard the feedback. My crew and I had endured extreme emotional stress to document something that not even *Whale Wars* had done and to expose a barbaric tradition that the world should stand against, that *Animal Planet* should stand against. To have that effort and that message crossed out in a network note was unacceptable. Rather than, "Oh my god. Good job. I can't believe you filmed this," we heard instead, "This is hard for our viewers to watch. It needs to go."

Mind you, when the town bell rang, we could have sat in our beautiful hotel, watched satellite TV, and had a beer, but we didn't. We went and shot this atrocity until 4:00 a.m. after fifty hours of travel, traumatizing ourselves in the process. As you might be able to tell, I was furious. But even though I was pacing around in something approaching a blind rage, I managed to compose myself. I wrote a nice letter to the network, scheduled a call, and fought to keep the footage in the episode. They continued to push back, telling me that my show was a happy show and that we couldn't have bad things in there. I had to fight with everyone, even Patrick, but I dug in my heels against everyone who hadn't been in the field. They couldn't bear to look at it, but we knew it had to be seen. Eventually, I prevailed, and the episode turned out to be one of our lowest-rated episodes of the season. The metrics even showed that people tuned out right as the whales started swimming into the bay. I hate to say this, but the network was right. They weren't right to remove the story, but they were correct that viewers were so jaded that they weren't willing to sit through and care about real things happening around the world.

But—and this "but" is important—though many viewers tuned out, those who stuck with the episode were more likely to be appalled and energized by what they saw. The episode made a difference. Multiple petitions started as a result, creating awareness, spreading the message, and generating more headlines. The viewers who mattered to me most—not the ones who want to see only happy things and adventure and cowboy hats, but the ones who are going to read this book, the people who support me—they tuned in and said, "This is an abomination. This is horrible. I didn't know this existed." Then they did something about it. The movement wasn't huge, no. It didn't create change in the Faroe Islands. It didn't stop the grind. But it made hundreds of thousands more people aware. So, although I lost some viewers on that episode, I wouldn't do a thing differently. I'd fight just as hard to get that on the air.

This was also when I realized that the network cared more about ratings than it did about conservation. Again, knowing what I know now, this shouldn't come as a surprise. But, at the time, I believed that Animal Planet would know when to take a stand, when their mission purpose would override market concerns. That they did not, that they fought to remove even five minutes of uncomfortable viewing, was a tough pill for me to swallow. I don't make this point to single out Animal Planet. There is no person there to blame. My partners at the network have made me into who I am today and have supported me in many ways. But the system is broken. The fact is that History channel has very little to do with history and Shark Week is more about Shaq than sharks. To expect that a network would transcend that market, succeeding on noble ideas alone, is naïve. I began then to accept that television actually limited the message I could tell. I could sing a happy song, so to speak, all day long. But the executives would keep the sadness away because no one would watch it. And I am certain that if you walked up to an Animal Planet executive today and asked what was more important to the network, animals or ratings, he or she would make no bones about telling you that ratings ruled.

This was a difficult passage for me as a television host and as a conservationist. We had encountered untold ugliness in the Faroe Islands and then had to fight to share that bad news with the world. The conservation problems were real and pressing, and the tool I had to combat them was imperfect. It felt as if we had lost the battle, but the challenge only redoubled our efforts to win the war. We were motivated to build upon what we had done in season one, when we made the impossible possible with the Zanzibar leopard, and to do it again and again. Although television was an imperfect medium, it was nevertheless a powerful one, a privileged one, and something I would need to extract the maximum value from in season two of *Extinct or Alive*. There were still people out there who would rather kill and destroy than feel and help, so I had to push my message harder and further than ever. To do so, however, a brief clip from a trail camera wasn't going to cut it. I needed to hold these lost animals in my hands, to prove to the world they existed and deserved protection, so they wouldn't end up like that baby pilot whale on the beach, dying without anyone even knowing.

CARTELS,
JUNGLE
POWDER,
AND
CAIMAN

CARTELS, JUNGLE POWDER, AND CAIMAN

aving seen what wild animals were up against, we were even more focused for season two of *Extinct or Alive*. We came up with yet another ambitious list of target species, some of which had seemingly disappeared into some of the remotest terrain on the face of the earth. I had to get my hands on some new animals to reiterate our message that there was still so much to save. I was excited to begin our search for the Rio Apaporis caiman, a seven-foot-long crocodilian that hadn't been seen in forty years. For reasons of politics and geography, it was an animal that had a decent chance of being alive, and the expedition to find it was a perfect example of the lengths to which my crew and I go to create forty-four minutes of impactful television.

The lead-up to the expedition for the Rio Apaporis caiman was familiar. We researched the animal and its habitat.
We negotiated through fixers, arranged travel, and prepared to
transport an absurd amount of camera, camping, and survival
equipment into one of the far-flung corners of the world. We
were preparing to travel deep into FARC-controlled jungle
of the western Amazon. (FARC is the Revolutionary Armed
Forces of Colombia—People's Army.) We ran (and ignored—a
recurring theme you'll have noticed) a risk assessment that
firmly recommended canceling the expedition. Our chances
of being kidnapped were pegged at greater than 60 percent.

A special concern this time around was whether to inform the FARC rebels that we would be coming. As ever,
the human element was proving to be the hardest to predict.
Our thinking went that if we reached out ahead of time, they
could turn us down, conveying the old, "Don't come—or we
will kill you," effectively squashing any chance of finding this
animal. Then again, the idea of a blundering troupe of gringos,
slogging film equipment through the jungle at night trying to
sneak past them didn't hold much appeal either. So, through
our fixer, we decided to give advance notice of our intentions
and hope for the best.

"We're not there to film them. We're looking for this crocodile. Please grant us access. Please don't kidnap or murder us."

After some back and forth, the verdict came back from
the FARC leadership.

"Okay, but don't screw us over," or words to that effect.

Surprisingly, we never even had to discuss a bribe. Maybe these FARC guys were really all about peace, love, and understanding?

Having appeased the local commandos, at least for the moment, I thought we would be in the clear to run our expedition as necessary. However, our time in the Amazon would prove daunting not only for the general logistics of travel (think *River of Doubt* but on a schedule), but for the seemingly insignificant obstacles that surprised us along the way. In this case, after months of burning through man hours and money, the surprise obstacle was not some FARC patrol flipping us from our hammocks, but a monkey bone about the size of my thumb.

Let me explain.

In January 2019, I boarded the flight from Los Angeles to Bogotá with my crew of five, my traveling fraternity, as Jessica had come to call it. We were incredibly excited at the prospect of venturing into a part of the Amazon where no Westerner had likely ever been. It was that same feeling we had on our trip to Myanmar for *Face the Beast*. We arrived in Bogotá, the capital city of Colombia, which is a colorful, vibrant, and cosmopolitan place. But there is also a distinct scent of violence in the air. I wondered what it might portend for our trip into the jungle. After catching a short night of sleep in a hotel, we piled into a minivan and drove six hours to a private airport where we boarded a Douglas DC-3, a rugged airplane, a popular model since the 1930s that is often referred to as "a collection of parts flying in loose formation."

Our plane may have actually been from the 1930s and seemed to be enjoying a late career transporting cargo to and from dirt landing strips in the middle of the Colombian Amazon. Its cargo is obvious to anyone who has ever watched *Narcos*. We ignored the implications, said our private prayers, and loaded two cases of personal belongings and camping equipment and then twelve cases of camera gear into the plane. We flew two hours over nothing but green jungle and brown rivers, shuddering along with our equipment in the ancient fuselage, until finally landing in the tiny village of Villa Gladys. The pilots told us they had never landed there before. I wasn't sure whether I believed them. But we were certainly the first white people to have visited the village in generations, if ever.

We took the steps down from the DC-3 to the landing. The village consisted of several small crop fields and nine thickly walled huts. About fifty people had come out to watch our plane land. The villagers appeared stern, maybe because they didn't know what to make of us. So, in a preemptive strike of diplomacy, we brought our bags of Jolly Ranchers and started handing them out. Children love candy no matter where you go, and the children of Villa Gladys had probably never had refined sugar in their lives. They loved it, yelling in delight as they chased after one another. Even so, the adult villagers, though polite, remained reserved and quiet. We didn't know how they viewed our arrival. We didn't know what the FARC may have told them. We arrived late enough in the day that we had no choice but to spend the night before continuing upriver the next morning. We set up our hammocks in the middle of the village.

On my phone, I had black-and-white photos, taken in the early 1970s, of the Rio Apaporis caiman. The animal had an incredible, elongated snout that was distinct from other native caiman species. In the luxuriant late-afternoon light, I walked around the village, showing these pictures to anyone curious enough to meet with me (and check out my iPhone), communicating in my terrible Spanish. The villagers mainly spoke an Indian dialect, and their Spanish was about as good as mine. I asked if they had seen a "big nose" caiman.

"Si."

"What about black caimans?"

"Si."

"Yellow caimans?"

"Si."

Everything was yes. The first few confirmations had been exciting, but by the end of my questioning I wasn't feeling any more confident than before.

We had planned to leave early the next morning but learned that the canoes we had arranged for were not there. We would have to wait another whole day before heading upriver. This was no reason to panic. This was just how expeditions often unfolded. Unlike some of the showrunners I have worked with in the past, we didn't take it for granted that we were operating far afield alongside cultures with totally different mindsets. This was the Amazon, not a soundstage. But, as we were burning time, wandering about the village, a man I had spoken to earlier delivered an undeniable warning.

"You can't go up the river to these big-nosed caiman. You will die."

Again, I had heard this kind of talk from time to time. I expected to be told the rebels were up there and if they found us, they would kill us. But this was not the case.

"You must listen. The spirits will kill you if you haven't been cleansed."

Now, I probably don't need to remind you that I am a scientist. I don't believe that spirits hold my fate in their ethereal hands any more than you do, but I did need to appease this villager before being allowed to travel ahead to my goal. I asked what I needed to do to be cleansed.

"You have to meet Lorenzo. He is the village elder. He can tell you whether or not you can go."

"Okay, great," I said, "Well, where is Lorenzo?"

"You can't see Lorenzo until after dark."

How convenient, I thought, that we were stuck here anyway. I was told Lorenzo had invited us to visit his *maloca*, or his shaman's hut, the traditional seat of power in small communities like this one. We waited until night began to fall. Shadows seemed to rush out from the surrounding jungle, the din of insects was taking over the night, and the smell of campfire drifted along the pathways between the huts. As we made our way to the maloca, villagers urged us to partake in a muddy brown liquid, poured from a gasoline canister, that was being passed around in a single wooden cup. We were all asked to drink.

It was fermented and revolting, probably a measure stronger than the scud that the farm workers drank in Zimbabwe. Once properly fortified, we were led to Lorenzo's maloca. It was the biggest building in the village, a huge, thatched, rudimentary structure. No concrete. No plywood. The building was made entirely from the jungle. It was open to the air on all four sides, and four fires burned beneath its roof. It had been made clear to us that our visit wasn't mandatory. We could go upriver. No one would physically stop us. But if we did, we would die. To the locals, this was a simple statement of fact, and Lorenzo was the only person who might grant us safe passage.

As we entered, a beautiful old man—short, muscular, broad through his bare chest and shoulders—beckoned us to sit by the main fire. It was, of course, Lorenzo himself. The six of us found our place, and I began to ask him questions. How long had he lived in the jungle? How many children did he have? How many wives? What animals did he like to hunt? What plants did he like to grow? The process of communication went slowly, until finally, Lorenzo said, "I would like to invite you to go up the river."

This was good. This was what we had come here for. But there was no forcing the conversation even from this point forward. The average well-meaning person might have sat down by the fire and immediately stated his or her intentions to travel upstream and capture a caiman. They might have asked in the friendliest way for Lorenzo's blessing, but without an understanding of the respect and time required to build trust, a direct request would have led nowhere.

"Lorenzo," I said, "We would like that very much. We're looking for the caiman amarilla. Trumpa largo. The big-nosed yellow caiman."

"Yes, I believe it is up the river, very far up the river. But it is very dangerous up there. There are very bad spirits, and no one goes there."

"I understand, Lorenzo, but I must go. I must find this animal. It is very important to me. What can I do to find it?"

"Who is going?"

"Everyone here," I gestured to my crew. "All these gringos are going to look for this caiman."

"Okay. Then what you have to do is you must be blessed."

"Lorenzo, can I ask you for the respect of being blessed, being protected to go up the river?"

Lorenzo furrowed his brow at this last request. I had the sense that he didn't know if this was okay. This was the first time white people had ever been in his maloca, the first time they had sat around his fire, and the first time they had asked to venture fifty miles into an area to which he himself wouldn't travel. Yet, eventually, he said yes.

To administer the blessing, he offered us *chopa*, yet another new substance. I didn't (and don't) know what chopa was other than a green powder contained within a snail shell that was sealed with bee's wax. Lorenzo handed the snail shell to Trevor (my Australian soundman who, ever since Myanmar, had become a staple for adventures), along with a V-shaped, hollowed-out monkey bone. He instructed Trevor to place a small amount of chopa into one end of the monkey bone and to place that same end in his nostril. The other end of the monkey bone went into Trevor's mouth. Then he told Trevor to blow. Trevor did, and his face turned bright red, his eyes teared, and sweat began to drip down his neck. He then gamely completed the ritual with his other nostril.

"What's it like?" I asked.

"It's like someone poured chlorine on your brain."

I didn't know what that meant. The snail shell passed to Johnny, then to Mitchell. They each reacted the same way, experiencing some kind of unpleasant rush but otherwise remaining upright and coherent. I was getting nervous. I don't do drugs—not then and not now. I don't write this for the public relations value. I wouldn't break a sweat if I had five cobras coiled before me. But this random green powder had my heart racing as it was passed my way. Lorenzo handed me the monkey bone, his face perfectly impassive in the fire-thrown shadows of his hut. I filled one end with chopa, situated that end in my nostril, and then blew quick and hard into the other.

In an instant, my lungs seized up. It felt as if acid were searing the coils of my brain. But I had to complete the ritual and willed myself to reload and fire into my other nostril. The prefrontal cortex of my brain, where the bridge of your nose meets your forehead, felt as if it were being reduced into a fiery liquid. My heart pounded. My vision tunneled. I had this terrible feeling of being unable to take a breath. Chopa was bad, I thought! For whatever reason, I felt the need to stand to find more air, to move away from this horrible sensation. Instead, I buckled to my knees and forearms and then, remaining in the position, vomited explosively onto the ground. Even though I was far from well, I was mainly worried that I had profoundly offended Lorenzo. Here he had asked me to partake in a sacred rite, and there I was puking it back out at the edge of the fire.

"I am so sorry, Lorenzo. I don't mean to be disrespectful. Please understand."

I spoke to our translator, Tomas, "Please, Tomas, tell Lorenzo to not be offended."

While I pleaded for his pardon and understanding, Lorenzo sat there stone-faced and still. The ceremony had come to a complete halt. The others were once again passing around the foul-smelling brown liquid, and I struggled to control my spasming gut. I was the only one who had reacted this way. I rejoined the circle about fifteen minutes later. My eyes were bloodshot, my brow a sweaty mess. I felt like I might start vomiting all over again. Then Lorenzo spoke for the first time since the start of my episode.

"Good." He cracked a smile.

"Good?"

"Yes, you were the one who was going to have the problem."

I was the one who dealt with the animals. My cameramen were fantastic at their jobs, but they're not wading neck-deep in a swamp to catch man-eating crocodiles. That's me, right?

"You were the one," he continued, "who was going to die, and you got the bad spirits out now. You will be safe. And you will be successful."

Cartels, Jungle Powder, and Caiman

We piled into three canoes the morning after the blessing. We invited several villagers to join us, but all fifty wanted to go. After politely whittling down our new companions to just a few, we motored upriver with no real destination in mind. There were beautiful sights everywhere: groups of primates, snakes in trees, and unbroken walls of foliage. We saw many caiman, though they were not the species we were looking for. After traveling most of the day, approximately fifty miles from the village, I told the crew to stop. We anchored and let the current pass us by on a stretch of water that looked about as promising as every other. It had the same color water, the same type of habitat, and the same kind of banks as dozens of similar stretches that we had already passed. While it was late afternoon, we still had daylight and could have puttered on for another two hours before making camp. But I was feeling uncommonly sure of myself (yes, even more so than usual). Maybe Lorenzo's assurance that no harm would come to me enabled me to trust my instinct a bit more freely. I can't attest to the spiritual power of his blessing, but there was an undeniable psychological effect.

We built camp, hung our hammocks, and made dinner. The lads and I had now been traveling for more than sixty hours. We looked pretty rough. We could all have used a break, but the objective was just ahead of us, and the anxiety of not knowing what came next had us shoveling down our food. Once the sun set, I announced to the crew, "It's time to find our caiman."

Did I really expect to find our animal on the very first night? I didn't think we'd get that lucky. But it was possible. Searching with a flashlight from the bow of a canoe, I saw a dozen sets of eyes shine. At night, when hit with a beam of light, the lens in the back of a crocodile's eye reflects a bright, orange-red glow. I knew there were other species in the area, so we steered the canoe to each set of shining eyes to identify them. We seemed to be surrounded by them.

"Okay, this is a dwarf caiman . . . Okay, this is a smooth-fronted caiman . . ."

We were clearly in an ecosystem that supported healthy populations of crocodilians, just not the one we were looking for. Then, farther away, I saw a larger set of eyes, much larger, actually, the size of golf balls, glowing red like dragon eyes.

"That's a bigger animal."

We approached those red eyes, but before we came within thirty-five feet, they disappeared. Believe it or not, this was unusual. In fact, I had never had this happen before. Crocodiles don't have many natural predators, and they aren't as skittish as you might think. I had caught saltwater crocodiles, Nile crocodiles, American alligators, and close to every other species of caiman that existed. I had developed a nearly foolproof approach to capturing these most dangerous reptiles. I knew how to be quiet, what angles to take, which ones to grab, which ones to noose. But never had I encountered a crocodilian that was so wary, so skittish that in the middle of a jungle, where no human had ventured within this animal's lifetime, that it disappeared at my barest approach. I watched the "footprint," or the wake, it left behind. I observed the length of the snout print as the animal sank under. I knew that I had just seen an extinct species of caiman, an animal the world had not seen in forty years. The only problems were that I had no evidence and my crew didn't believe me. I didn't blame them. It takes a lot of practice to discern the difference in caiman species, especially from a distance. I had my years of training as a tracker and my understanding of the animal's morphology (mixed with a little bit of gut instinct) to support a firm hunch.

"How can you tell? It looks just like every other one," Mitch said, speaking for the group.

I started to doubt my own eyes. There was no other option but to catch our animal. For the next seven nights, we tried and failed. We saw several of what we thought were Rio Apaporis caiman, which was potentially a feat unto itself, to discover a thriving population of an extinct species. We just couldn't get close enough to catch one. We were learning that it was an intelligent and highly elusive animal. Combine those traits with its habitat, a tract of jungle patrolled by armed rebels, and there was a good explanation for why no one had seen the Rio Apaporis in decades. The search was made more difficult by the sheer number of other caiman species that continued to distract our attention. We were dealing with a needle in a haystack in the middle of the FARC-controlled Colombian Amazon, and my crew still didn't see what I saw.

I tried to catch them with my hands, with snares (safe for the animal), and with nets (not safe for the crew). I tried hiking along the banks and jumping down upon them. No luck. But my team was beginning to believe and started to identify our target species based on its behavior. Then, while stalking along the bank, approaching yet another pair of promising eyes, I spotted an eighteen-foot-long anaconda. The adrenaline kicked in.

"Drop your camera and help me!" I shouted to Mark.

The snake began to glide away from us, down the bank and farther into the water. I dove in and grabbed the animal by the tail. Bad idea. I was hoping this animal had recently fed on a Rio Apaporis caiman and had caiman DNA in its feces. The biome of its gut content could be my genetic proof that the caiman exists! The snake lunged out of the water, snapping at me, then dove back toward the river, pulling me with it. I was quickly losing this fight. Mark grabbed on. The whole team seemed to appear at once. Five of us, with one cameraman filming, worked to loosen the anaconda's grip on a tree trunk about three feet under the water. The snake was so strong, so smooth, it was like holding onto a greased hose of pure muscle. The snake again reversed course to attack us. I maneuvered out of the way and Mark, who is also a herpetologist, grabbed the snake behind the head and subdued it. I located the animal's cloacal area and, right on cue, it crapped all over my arm.

I thought of what I might tell my producers at Animal Planet.

"Well, I went to the Amazon against all of your wishes and at great expense, didn't catch the animal, didn't get footage, but I did bring home this jar of snake shit."

It rained for the next four days, stalling any attempts we might have made to collect any evidence besides feces. Several of our cameras failed. We ate boiled piranha and jungle fruit for every meal. Our morale was approaching its low point. But my belief in our eventual success was still bright. Maybe there really was something to Lorenzo's blessing.

On the tenth day of our expedition, the rain finally stopped. We didn't waste time and returned to the canoes. For whatever reason, maybe because this was the first break in the rain for days, the wasps were out. They seemed to be drawn to the lights in our canoes, which we couldn't risk turning off because we would ride right onto the bank. So, every twenty seconds or so someone would shout, having just been stung. These weren't normal wasps, either. They were parasitic wasps known for their highly painful venom. I was stung and stung again, eleven times in total on the first post-rain patrol. The situation was becoming untenable. Then Mitch tapped me on the shoulder.

"Forrest, I'm not feeling so good."

Mitch had been stung like the rest of us. But unlike anyone else, his face was completely puffed up. His eyes were almost shut. He was wheezing. He was going into anaphylactic shock. This was as dangerous a situation as we had faced during any of our expeditions. As ever, we were days from anything resembling a hospital or clinic. Josh, our medic, took a look at Mitch.

"We are in trouble. Big trouble."

We sped back to camp to retrieve an EpiPen from the medical supply. Josh jabbed the device into Mitch's leg, shooting a dose of epinephrine into his bloodstream. We waited, watching and listening, for any improvement in Mitch's condition. And thank God, a few minutes later, his airways began to unconstrict. His wheezing subsided. It was working. Mitch had a handy supply of epinephrine to thank for recovering so quickly from the wasp stings. He also had himself to thank for remaining calm throughout the whole ordeal, keeping his heart rate steady to slow the spread of the wasp venom and the rate of anaphylaxis.

We were soaked, stung, and exhausted, having been fueled by little more than boiled piranha, which really loses its luster after a day or two. It was about 2:00 a.m. We had been working since 7:00 the previous morning. Mitch was recovering in a tent, having been brought back from the brink. But the mission remained at hand.

"Right. Who's ready to go back out?"

Johnny, our assistant camera operator, was the only one to volunteer. Everyone else was wiped out and justifiably so. There were no hard feelings. They needed the rest. Johnny and I headed back to the river, dazed ourselves from wasp stings and lack of sleep.

With sunrise brushing light on the horizon, I spotted a final glint of eyeshine on a distant bank. I saw a pair of golf ball–sized dragon eyes, glowing red. This had to be the same seven-foot-long animal we had seen the very first night. This was the moment when karma and perseverance lined up. Johnny and I were silent. We didn't speak and didn't need to. We knew the routine, had gone through these motions hundreds of times in the previous few days. And we knew we had to be perfect right there and then. I reached my hand back. Johnny flipped the catch pole into my grip. I pointed forward as Johnny steered the canoe right where I needed to go. I raised my hand in a blocking motion and the canoe stopped silently. For the first time in more than a week, a Rio Apaporis caiman sat motionless upon our approach.

"This is the one," I whispered to myself and reached with the catch pole just as the animal exploded forward into the noose, cinching the rope beyond its jawline. I pulled back and screamed.

"I've got him, Johnny!"

With Johnny's help, I dragged the caiman onto the bank and wrestled it in ankle-deep water and mud. Johnny held the tail with one hand and a flashlight with the other while filming. (Johnny once stopped a bull shark from killing me when my back was turned. He's a man of many talents.) It was a calamitous moment, but eventually we got the animal under control and could begin our work.

We took photos, measurements, and samples of blood and feces. Then we let the caiman go. At camp, we woke everyone up right as the sun was rising. There was nothing but excitement and celebration. Mitch, in his epinephrine-induced stupor, clapped my shoulder.

"I knew we would do it."

That same day we packed up and headed downstream to Villa Gladys.

I can barely describe the mixture of relief and excitement I felt. We had done it again. Through sheer force of will, with my team by my side, we had achieved the impossible twice. First the Zanzibar leopard, now the Rio Apaporis caiman. The genetic material I collected from the specimen confirmed that the samples were, indeed, from the Rio Apaporis caiman, essentially pulling a seven-foot-long crocodilian from the black maw of extinction. Astoundingly, after further analysis, we learned that not only did we prove the existence of the Rio Apaporis caiman, but we had the evidence to support an entirely new species. The Rio Apaporis had long been considered a subspecies of the far more abundant spectacled caiman. But the data collected from our expedition met the criteria to describe a new species altogether. Under the evolutionary species concept, the scientific standard used for species delineation, the specimen had a unique evolutionary lineage dating back 5 million to 7 million years. For the past 200 years, the scientific consensus had been that there were approximately twenty-four species of crocodilians. Now there were potentially twenty-five.

The impact of the discovery was staggering, and I loved the way we did it. We were willing to venture into the unknown, into danger, into an inaccessible pocket of the world where most sane people would never think of going. We demonstrated our commitment to the cause and came back triumphant. But before the proverbial champagne could flow, we had a decision to make. On one hand, we wanted to crow to the world about what we had risked and how we had been rewarded. We wanted to preach for conservation dollars. On the other, we wondered whether we should tell anyone at all. In a rare turn, this animal had been *protected* by humanity's ignorance. FARC rebels had kept everyone away. We had penetrated a Garden of Eden of sorts and had plucked one of its rarest fruits. What would happen once everyone knew it was there?

The debate of whether to go public was one of convenience in this case. How many other humans were willing to follow in our footsteps? I bet not many. More importantly, by following the example of scientists such as Ha Hoang, studying Rafetus turtles in Vietnam; Bill Robichaud, seeking saola in Laos; and Charlie Berger, chasing wolves in northern Canada, we knew the right thing to do was to inform the Western world of this discovery for the greater scientific good.

And the good was about to become great.

THE NEW POSTER CHILD
OF CONSERVATION

THE NEW POSTER
CHILD OF
CONSERVATION

I don't want to downplay the significance of finding a Rio Apaporis caiman, because it was fantastic. But the re-discovery of the species took place in a part of the Amazon that no Westerner had been to in thirty years. The Rio Apaporis caiman was never necessarily believed to be extinct. It was just missing. No scientist had been able to travel to the region safely for decades. Our expedition had benefited from a change in the political winds when the Colombian government and the FARC negotiated a peace deal in 2017. But, as for the Fernandina Island tortoise, a giant tortoise on the Galápagos Islands, there was no question. It was extinct.

STILL ALIVE

At the start of season two, Patrick had asked me where I wanted to go. Never mind my chances of finding an extinct animal there, what was my dream destination? It took only a second for the Galápagos Islands to appear in my mind, and the idea of locating a lost giant tortoise on the islands that Darwin made famous was the stuff of fantasy. Patrick readily agreed. *Extinct or Alive* would be going to the Galápagos in season two. But I felt like there was something I needed to do first, somewhere else that I had to see. So, before we took a trip to those equatorial islands, I brought my crew back home to southern Africa, or what had been home, in search of the Cape lion, a black-maned giant that once hunted the elephant migration from South Africa to Zimbabwe. If you've seen the episode, you'll recall that it was on this trip that Mitch had his encounter with the black rhino, when he held steady enough to save us all. It was also on this trip that I brought Mitch and Johnny to my old farm.

When our plane touched down in Harare, I couldn't resist making the offer. I asked whether Mitch and Johnny would come with me. I wanted and didn't want to see what was there now and figured I could use the company. They knew that I had been kicked out of my home at gunpoint, they knew what the feeling was toward white landowners in Zimbabwe, and they understood the risks involved with returning to a farm from which you had been forcibly removed. But neither one would let me do this alone. They grabbed their smallest cameras and hopped into the car. The memory of the route hadn't deserted me, and I knew exactly where we were going. I turned onto the rough road that led to the gate, which had once been the beautiful entrance to the property but was now broken and dilapidated. It was the same gate that I had passed through fifteen years earlier in the back seat of my mother's car, crying as I waved goodbye to my friends and my dogs. I started to get nervous then. I didn't know I was capable of being nervous. Anyone who catches poisonous snakes and giant crocodiles for a living doesn't have much use for anxiety or doubt. I had been scared, certainly, but not nervous, not like this. A lump formed in my throat, the hair stood up on my arms, and, for what seemed like the first time in my life, I was being wrapped in a scratchy cloth of anxiety.

I knew I had to play it cool. We were white strangers who were trespassing. As we continued down the drive, I saw that the hundred-year-old trees had been cut, the fig tree where my mom tied up that man and I shot him in the leg was gone, the dam where I spent the happiest days of my childhood was a muddy patch, and the swimming pool had been drained and filled with what looked and smelled like goat shit. The house came into view and the windows were all smashed. The place had been destroyed.

A man name Mr. Mbafu came out to meet us.

"Who are you? What are you doing here?"

He was clearly very suspicious of us. I answered him.

"I used to live here and just wanted to come and see it."

He pointed at Mitch in the car.

"He looks like a reporter."

Mitch stepped out of the car to shake Mr. Mbafu's hand, trying to put him at ease. Reporters weren't welcome visitors in Zimbabwe. International coverage of land reform had been almost universally negative. Mr. Mbafu wasn't eager to make any headlines. But we managed to joke with him enough that he allowed us to tour the property.

If you've watched the episode, you'll know this was a tough moment for me. Seeing my family's land in such a dilapidated state was hard to process. All the things from my childhood that I remembered as being so perfect and so beautiful and so pure were all shattered and ruined and damaged. Standing down by the pool, I took a video with my phone of the land.

"Hey Mom, look where I am."

When I showed her the video, she recognized the land but saw that it was unalterably changed. In a way, I wish I had never revisited the farm. In another, I am so glad that I did. The fantasy of my incredible childhood was gone. It didn't exist any longer. I wasn't going to raise my son there in the same way I had been raised. I wasn't going to fight for my land like I'd always wanted to and take it back. The trees had been felled. And this life, this memory, was all gone. Mitch and Johnny stayed with me during that heavy moment. They saw that it was hard. They captured it. And then they picked me back up and charged with me toward the rest of the adventures awaiting us during the filming of season two.

◇ ◇ ◇

ONLY ONE SPECIMEN OF THE FERNANDINA ISLAND GIANT TORTOISE had ever been found—and that was 114 years ago. In 1906, the California Academy of Sciences came across an animal, which, of course, they killed straightaway to keep as a specimen. So, in the entirety of recorded human history, only one individual of the species had ever been found. I spoke with friends of mine at the Turtle Conservancy in Ojai, California, and met with a man named Ross Kiester. He told me that he had traveled to the island in the 1960s and found bite marks on a cactus, and that those bite marks could only have been from a tortoise. He had also found tortoise scat. This man's entire life centered on the study of chelonians, so his report could be taken seriously. Considering that tortoises live upwards of one hundred years, the animal that had snacked on that cactus could still be alive. This was compelling stuff. Ross recalled that he had found the bite marks on top of a mountain, which had been incredibly difficult to get to and would require a helicopter if we planned to film a television program there. I went to work, trying to find a helicopter. But there were none to be found in the Galápagos, and to bring one from mainland Ecuador would have cost millions of dollars, money we did not have. We would have to rely on good old footwork.

I reached out to the Galápagos National Parks and the Galápagos Conservancy, the two major organizations that oversaw scientific work on the islands. We told them about our mission to search for the Fernandina Island tortoise and requested permits to land there. (No tourists are allowed on the island except for a small landing area that affords visitors a view of a scorching moonscape of volcanic rock.) As luck would have it, a biologist named Washington Tapia worked at the Galápagos Conservancy and thought we weren't totally out of our minds.

"I believe that there's a chance, an unlikely one, but a chance that the Fernandina Island tortoise is still on the island," he told us. "It's a giant island. It's largely unexplored, and even though I've been there five or six times and have never seen one, I think it could be there."

Following these promising developments, we traveled to the Galápagos to interview the head of the Galápagos Conservancy to see what he thought about our search. His outlook was not as encouraging. Smirking smugly for our camera, he told us the tortoise was long gone, that we didn't have a chance, and that we were wasting our time. I thanked him for the vote of confidence, wished him luck, and left. That interview never made the show because we didn't want to make him look like a dummy, but I'm happy for it to make the book.

The boat ride from Puerto Ayora to Fernandina Island took a full day. Washington Tapia and Jeffreys Malaga, another biologist from the Galápagos Conservancy, joined me and my crew to conduct the search. We made landfall on this incredible island, a jagged mound of dark, volcanic rock roasting in the sea, and were surrounded by basking and leaping animals. There were fur seals, gorgeous animals with giant doe-like eyes. There were huge green sea turtles sunbathing on the sand. And, on boulder after boulder, craggy marine iguanas clung to the rocks. It was like stepping back in time. These animals had no fear of humans, were not conditioned to seeing us, and lacked natural predators. You could walk right up to them. It was a stark and profound contrast to our relationship with animals everywhere else on the planet. Here was nature still in a primordial state.

Of course, we weren't there to look at seals and iguanas, which had been filmed by every other nature documentary that had ever visited the Galápagos. We were there to find something no camera had ever seen. Some people questioned whether this hidden jewel *ever* existed. And, as ever, the search wasn't going to be easy.

Soon after disembarking onto the island, we recorded the temperature at 122 degrees Fahrenheit. We needed to set up camp before committing to the search in earnest and spent half of the first day on the island constructing a base that would provide us with shade and shelter. We had porters whose only job was to run fresh water from the boat to the camp. Not only did we have to contend with the massive equatorial sun, but the island itself was an active volcano with near-constant lava flows. The ground was composed of four-foot-tall shards of lava-like glass. We had no choice but to walk across these jet-black, spiky rocks. Whether bipedal or quadrupedal, it made no difference, there was no way to make safe or steady progress through this terrain. We were working in an utter cauldron, and our boots literally melted beneath our feet.

But, even in these conditions, the prospect of discovery worked its magic, and we scoured the area for any clues. That same day, while walking in a dry wash, we spotted what could have been tortoise tracks. The series of little divots in rocky sand provided some hope that we might be looking in the right place, but the area was otherwise unpromising—no trees, no shade, little water. I sat down with Washington and Jeffreys to discuss our strategy, and we decided that the next day we needed to climb to the top of the mountain. By mountain they meant caldera, and it was huge. Our camp was near sea level and the volcano was approximately 4,800 feet in elevation. This was going to be a haul.

The mountain was promising because of the condensation at higher elevation that helped support more plant life. We woke up the next morning, had a quick breakfast of granola bars and coffee, slapped on our backpacks, and started our hike. The early hours were relatively pleasant. We were walking through a gradually greening slope. Then the sun crested the ridgeline and the brutality resumed. Washington, Jeffreys, and I distracted ourselves from the heat by going over Ross's find from the 1960s and why that was a plausible sighting. Washington shared rumors that planes flying over the island had spotted suspiciously rounded boulders that very well could have been tortoises. We were having a grand old time, just three biologists in this incredible environment, hiking up and up. We found a fossilized piece of what I think was a sea turtle shell. We ran into a few land iguanas and Galápagos hawks. However, there were no signs that tortoises were actively living along the slope of the mountain. Later in the day, as we reached about 1,200 feet in elevation, I turned back toward the ocean, looked down toward the west, and spotted a patch of green near the coastline. I turned to Washington and Jeffreys.

"There's a patch of real vegetation down there," as opposed to the sparse and sporadic shrubs and grasses we had been walking through all that day. "I think we should head down in that direction."

"No, no, no. That's too low in elevation. There's not enough water." Washington and Jeffreys agreed that it wasn't the right habitat.

"You might be right," I told them, "but my instinct says that if you want to find the animal, you need to find the cover on an island, like what's down there. That's the only place that I can see a tree anywhere."

But the local biologists prevailed in this case, and we continued to climb higher for the remainder of the first day. We headed back to camp without any kind of sighting and arrived there in pitch darkness at 9:00 or 10:00 at night, and the temperature still hovered near one hundred degrees. We were sitting around having a dinner of granola bars when I spoke up about a new search area.

"Guys, tomorrow I want to head to that green patch."

"No, I don't think it's possible. There's a huge lava flow between here and there. It'll be very, very difficult. Also, it's the wrong elevation. The tortoise won't be there."

So, a little bit of an argument followed, totally polite and diplomatic, and I made the point that we got to do their thing today, so tomorrow we'd do mine, and we can alternate the decision-making until our time is up. This seemed to satisfy everyone, and we tucked in for a very uncomfortable sleep.

The hike was as bad as Washington and Jeffreys had predicted. We woke up predawn and crossed the lava flow over the course of six or seven hours. Maybe we covered two-and-a-half miles in that time. At every step we'd break through a sharp crust of volcanic rock. We had to weave in and out of the towering shards of basalt that had flared and been pushed vertical by subsequent volcanic activity. The pace was excruciatingly slow and only made worse by the blazing sun directly overhead. Eventually, I dropped down into the green valley that persisted between the twenty-foot-high lava flows. It was this isolated channel of life and trees that had maintained a foothold between the ever-expanding fields of basalt.

I was the first one to arrive, along with my camera crew. The hike over had spaced us apart, and Washington and Jeffreys were twenty or thirty minutes behind. The moment I dropped down into this verdant swath, the temperature dropped fifteen degrees. Even the shade of a sparse tree was a relief in such an exposed island. Within thirty seconds of entering this new zone, I spotted a Galápagos racer, an incredible snake, a species made famous by *Planet Earth II*, which captured the snakes as they chased newborn iguanas. The snake was one of several good signs. Iguanas moved through the underbrush. A hawk flew overhead. And as the old saying goes, you never leave fish to find fish. Or, in other words, life attracts life. That is a fact that holds true wherever you are. I knew then that we had located the most promising habitat we had seen over the previous three days. Twenty minutes later I saw a piece of dung. Shaking, I dropped to my knees.

The New Poster Child of Conservation

As many of my close friends could tell you, there are very few things that excite me as much as poop. Sitting before me, plopped in the dirt for all to see, was a moist, fist-sized piece of poop. Iguanas were the only other animal on the island that made leavings of any size. But iguana dung was long, skinny, and cylindrical. What rested before me was football shaped. I have two giant sulcata tortoises at home and knew what I was looking at.

"Oh my god. This is tortoise poop."

I jumped on the walkie-talkie.

"Jeffreys, Washington, where are you guys?"

"We're close! We're just getting to the green spot."

"Come right here. I'll holler for you."

Moments later they came busting through the brush.

I was pacing as I pointed at the dung and the area immediately around it.

"Look at that. See how there's something broken here. See how this belly drags right through here. Here's another piece of poop! It's older, but still tortoise."

They started getting excited. An energy was building among all of us. Washington took a long look at the dung.

"You're right, you're right, this is tortoise, this is tortoise."

I said, "Confirmed, Washington, this is not iguana poop, right? I'm not going crazy. I've seen a million iguanas. I've seen a million tortoises. This is tortoise poop?"

"One hundred percent."

"Is this old or new? It looks new. It's still wet."

"No, this is about a month old."

"Are you sure? It's really hot and dry here, but this is wet." I scooped tortoise poop from a cage every day when I was home. Again, I had more than a passing familiarity with the touch and feel of tortoise dung. But Washington insisted it was much older and the moisture could have come from rain or condensation. In any case, as the head producer of the show, I was thinking to myself, well, we've got our ending. We had proof in hand that there was a tortoise on the island. We had done it again. Here was another major discovery and another great episode to boot! But no one was slowing down. The energy was carrying everyone forward, searching through the rest of the green area. Then a few minutes later, Washington saw something else.

"There's a bed, there's a bed!"

I ran over from where I was playing with the poop. Giant tortoises bed down by digging a hole to get away from the scorching hot surface layer of sand and then plaster their belly on the cooler earth beneath. Sure enough, the bedding site was about 150 feet away from the dung. I tossed the clearly *fresh* poop over my shoulder to check out the bed. I was losing my mind at this point. Washington looked at the bed and changed his tune. It was new. We were back on the same page. We were on the trail of a living, breathing tortoise. We fanned out to scour the area. I will never forget that right as I was tilting my water bottle upward to take a drink, I heard Jeffreys shout, "Tortuga!" I tossed the hydro flask over my shoulder and dove into the bush like I was trying to tackle an escaping cheetah, which was ridiculous because this was a tortoise, the opposite animal. It had no speed and was going nowhere fast. The other scientists looked at each other, wondering what I was doing. But my instinct for quick action overwhelmed me. I dove into the bushes and emerged holding the Fernandina Island tortoise.

With the tortoise still in my arms, Washington sprung to my side and hugged me. And then Jefferys joined him. And then there we were, three sweaty men, hugging with a giant tortoise sandwiched between us. We put her down and were so overjoyed that we began jumping up and down, clapping, and shouting, "Bravo, bravo, bravo," which was a word we all understood. You might imagine collaborating scientists shaking hands in a sober recognition of their contribution to human knowledge. We danced and hugged. The flood of emotion was more than anyone knew how to handle. We held the crown jewel of the Galápagos, the crown jewel of extinct animals. This was an animal that had been seen only once 114 years ago and was known to science from only one specimen. I was holding it in my hands, staring into the beautiful blue eyes of this pig-nosed, incredible female Fernandina Island tortoise.

Keep in mind that the Galápagos tortoise is the icon of conservation. Everybody knows the name Lonesome George for a reason. But with his death a few years earlier, I was now holding the biggest symbol of hope that existed in the wildlife kingdom. I could tell the global impact the discovery would make. However, we had some biology to attend to before we could start thinking about the grand implications. We calmed down to draw her blood and place a PIT chip (passive integrated transponder, a tracking chip) beneath her skin. Then we had a difficult decision to make. I made the case for keeping her in place. After all, she had a PIT tag and wasn't going anywhere. But Jeffreys and Washington were quick to see the better of that idea.

"We can't leave her for multiple reasons. One, she's malnourished and she's underweight. Two, nobody will believe us. And three, if we take her back, this is the physical proof we need to save the species. Maybe if we give her some water and some food, maybe she still has viable eggs that she can lay." Female tortoises can retain the sperm of mates for up to twenty years. "This is the chance to save the species."

I looked at Washington and Jeffreys and said, "You're damn right. As much as she belongs here, she will do better in the Fausto Llerena breeding facility." The same facility where Lonesome George had lived. So, we created a stretcher (you can tell stretchers are a theme with me) and readied to transport her to the boat. I radioed Mitch, who had remained on the boat this whole time, manning the drones for aerial footage.

"We found it!"

Mitch and the crew could hardly believe it. I told him to use the drone to find me and to bring the boat around to where the green patch met the water. While the boat made its way toward us, we had a gnarly hike to complete with a seventy-pound tortoise hanging between two branches. There was no gentle beach for the skiff to land on. If you've seen the episode, you'll know it was all rocks and waves. Somehow, in a sequence that almost seems like a dream now, I hoisted the tortoise onto my shoulder and got her into the boat. She was safe. The other scientists decided that we should let the tortoise hang out on the boat for a day, where she had food and water and would have ticks removed, while we headed back inland to search for another tortoise, hopefully a male. But before we went to continue our work, Mark Romanov made an important point.

"What are we going to call her? We can't call her Chelonoidis phantasticus. That's so impersonal."

We all sat there, thinking, until Mark answered his own question.

"Lonesome George was so famous 'cause he had the name Lonesome George. What if we called the Fernandina Island tortoise Fern? It's a beautiful name."

We all said, "Absolutely."

Fern was a beautiful animal, too. In fact, I have a painting of her hanging over my turtle tank at home.

We didn't find much in our extra day of searching and headed back to the boat because we had to get Fern back to the breeding facility as quickly as possible. The eight- or nine-hour ride there was one of the sweetest moments of my scientific career. My team and I had accomplished in four days what the Galápagos Conservancy and the Galápagos National Parks could not accomplish in 114 years. I don't mention this to beat my chest, but because it is perfectly true. With Fern in the boat, I felt like a world beater. I had proven the doubters wrong again. And right about the time I was wondering whether this was what it felt like to be a Beatle or a Rolling Stone, the captain of the boat approached me.

"Can I have a word with you?"

"Sure," I said and followed him up to his quarters. I had absolutely no idea what he wanted to talk to me about. We had hardly interacted up to that point because he was driving the boat and I was on the island, fondling tortoise turds.

"What's going on?" I asked.

"Listen to me," he said, "I have lived in the Galápagos my whole life. I know everybody that lives in the Galápagos. These guys are going to steal what you did."

"What? No, they wouldn't do that."

"They will. I know how these things work. The most important thing to a scientist in the Galápagos is his career, and this is the biggest discovery in the Galápagos since Charles Darwin."

"Wow," I said, "That's quite a statement."

"Just be careful."

I laughed at him. Though I liked his estimation of our accomplishment, there was no way what he was saying was true. I was on cloud nine at that point and probably my sixth beer. I wasn't about to entertain the warnings of some skeptic, so I disregarded the conversation. Everything was to be gained by collaboration. We all found Fern together. We had footage of everything—from my identifying the green patch to Jeffreys yelling, "Tortuga!" We had combined resources and expertise to accomplish something amazing for a species that now had a greater chance of survival. What was there to steal?

The New Poster Child of Conservation

We got back to shore, and there was a whole brigade waiting for us. Jeffreys and Washington had been on their cell and satellite phones as soon as they could, notifying the center that we were bringing the tortoise. Then, as we docked, the strangest thing happened. Jeffreys and Washington picked up the tortoise, got off the boat, and told me, "Stay here."

What were they trying to do?

"Nope, sorry, I'm not staying here. Mitch, come with me and bring a camera."

The joy and significance of the moment quickly cleared away any static between me and the scientists from the Galápagos. There was so much to celebrate—the resurrection of a species and the reimagination of its future. Together we brought the tortoise to the breeding center. A pen had been readied and sterilized. We put Fern down, and she walked straight over to her giant watering pool and just sat down. It could have been the first time she'd seen standing fresh water in years. Because she was so dehydrated, she drank and drank, even with all these strange humans standing around her, staring at her in wonder. She wouldn't leave the water for three days. Six weeks later, she would be seven pounds heavier. It seemed that we had found this animal right on the verge of losing her forever.

Now this isn't just me telling you it was big news; Fern was *big news*. I flew straight from the Galápagos to New York City for a press tour. *Forbes, Times, Newsweek, Entertainment Tonight,* and *National Geographic* all featured the discovery. The story made for easy copy: here was this kid from Santa

Barbara by way of Zimbabwe who had been defying academics and had now made the biggest biological discovery of the century. I told this same story over and over, about the last sighting in 1906, about the rugged volcanic islands, about the collaboration between myself and the team from the Galápagos Conservancy and the Galápagos National Parks. We had all the right ingredients to achieve something remarkable. Then one reporter asked, "What about the allegations by Washington Tapia that you're not even a scientist and you had no part of the expedition?"

I laughed, "Excuse me?"

"Yeah, it says here in the *Ecuador Times* that one of the scientists said that you're not a real scientist and you weren't even part of the expedition. You just showed up to take pictures."

I asked him whether he was joking. It sounded preposterous.

"That's a misprint," I told the reporter. "Someone has misinterpreted something."

But, sure enough, there it was in black and white, from Washington's mouth to the *Ecuador Times*.

I was puzzled and hurt. The news continued to trickle out, mainly attributed to Washington, whom I had bear-hugged thinking he was the nicest guy I'd ever met. Turns out, the captain on the boat was right. Washington had launched a needless media campaign against me to take full credit for the discovery. If it was that important to them, as the local biologists, they could have said so and taken the lead. Truly. I would have let them. I didn't care about making the discovery for *me*. I cared about the discovery for the animal. That said, I do want a discovery to make the greatest impact it can for the sake of the species and its habitat. By working together, we could help increase awareness of Fern, and more money could be raised from the United States. But Washington's stance in the media matched the Galápagos Conservancy's stance toward me generally. Our collaboration was over. My attempts to contact them about future expeditions or about sending the money I had raised for the conservation of tortoise habitat were met with silence. It turns out they launched two follow-up expeditions to Fernandina Island in search of a male, but neither were successful.

I wish I didn't have to tell that story. The claims that I had nothing to do with the discovery eventually faded away and were never picked up by major media. After all, everything was on film. But it's an important story to tell. It shows how the animals we are trying to protect rely on imperfect stewards: people. Ego can undermine collaboration. Personal ambition can derail partnerships. And even within the conservation community, the animals don't always come first.

Along that same line of thinking, my personal disappointment isn't the point, either. Even though I am not involved in return efforts to find more of that species, we effectively saved that animal. The Fernandina Island tortoise is a new poster child of conservation. A lot of caring, understanding, and passion has been generated as a result, and very good things will happen in the Galápagos because of it.

After all, I would never be able to manage any of the species from our expeditions in an ongoing fashion. I couldn't take care of leopards in Zanzibar or caiman in Colombia or tortoises in the Galápagos. I am just a mercenary over here. I'm the hide-and-seek champ. And once I've done my thing, I hand responsibility over to incredible scientists like Washington and Jeffreys and those who work at the Fausto Llerena breeding facility. I don't possess the skill set to manage a species back to a sustainable population. My skill set allows me to find things that don't want to be found. My discoveries are meant to be handed over to in-country scientists who will do the long and hard work over years to take care of that species. When everybody is on the same page, it's a beautiful thing. Like Fern.

SHARKS FOR WEEKS

SHARKS FOR WEEKS

I could not have imagined that the surprising and twisting path of my life would have led to the discovery of Fern. Saying you're going to make an impact on a global scale is one thing, actually doing it is another. Even though I could never go back to the farm in Zimbabwe, even though my mother would never return to her life as a bush guide, I had nevertheless centered my life on conservation and was finding a new way in the world. I could not have guessed that a stint on *Naked and Afraid* would be the first domino to fall in a line of unexpected opportunities that would lead me to triumph in the Galápagos. My instinct to jump into the unknown and to chase down the next challenge had been serving me well. A show that had initially been slated for Monster Week had conjured a new poster child of global conservation.

You can't argue with results.

But you can wonder where you go from there.

After the discovery in the Galápagos (coupled with several others from season two), there was a temptation to rest upon my laurels. I could have transitioned back to an agreeable academic job. I could have returned to the life of a working biologist, knowing that I had proven my point with the success of *Extinct or Alive*. But though I may have reached a plateau in what I could achieve scientifically, there were still a few mountains left to climb (or depths to sound) in the world of television.

As anyone could tell you, the summit of nature cable programming, at least in terms of sheer exposure, is Shark Week on the Discovery Channel. It has been around for as long as I have been alive. It is steroidal. It is the Super Bowl of wildlife on cable TV. It is reality television for the cartilaginous. And though I might have considered myself as a hotshot with *Extinct or Alive*, in truth, I was punching above my weight. Discovery relied on a select roster of trusted hosts and showrunners to produce Shark Week—and I hadn't received an invitation.

Still, terrestrial animals aren't the only ones that have gone missing from our world; many aquatic ones have as well. My grandfather, in fact, played a part in the discovery of the coelacanth, an ancient fish thought to be extinct for 66 million years. In the 1950s, he was living in Africa and went to the island of Comoros on vacation. There, in a fish market, he spotted this very odd looking fish, something that he had never seen before. Now, my grandfather was a war hero and a boxer, not a biologist. But he was struck enough to freeze and ship the ungutted specimen all the way to Salisbury, the capital of what was then Rhodesia. Curators there confirmed that my grandfather had discovered one of the first intact, non-rotted specimens of a coelacanth. So, at the very least, I would be carrying on a family tradition by taking my talents to the sea.

It was time to start thinking about season three, and I told Eric that I had a show idea for a lost shark episode. But I wanted to single out this idea and suggested that we talk to Discovery about doing something for Shark Week. He wasn't convinced. Shark Week had a pretty consistent brand (think Shaquille O'Neal in a shark cage), and I wasn't it. Eric flew from New York to Los Angeles for a meeting we had with Joe Schneier, head of development for Discovery, to brainstorm ideas. As we neared the office, Eric reminded me, "Don't pitch your shark show. Nobody wants to buy a show about a two-foot-long shark. They want jaws. They want teeth. They want attack. Okay?"

"Sure," I said.

I kept quiet as Eric and Joe bantered about tiger sharks, shark-attack victims, and flying great whites. I could see where this was going, and I could already feel the look Eric was giving me. He knew I was about to open my mouth and was willing me with the most forceful nonverbal communication he could muster to keep it shut. But as we have seen time and again in this book, I can't help myself.

"Joe, what do you think about *Extinct or Alive* for Shark Week?"

"What do you mean?"

"Well, around 1970, the Pondicherry shark completely vanished, and this is an animal that's barely been seen, a species with only a handful of archetype specimens in the world, and I reckon I can find it."

"Well, how big is it? Does it kill people? Is it a scary shark? I've never heard of this thing. Tell me about it."

"Oh, it's about two feet long, completely harmless, lives in both rivers and the ocean, like a bull shark, but couldn't be friendlier."

Joe paused to consider this.

"Well, that's not very good."

Eric glared at me.

"But . . . if you know anything about the Indian Ocean," I went on, "the locations where it occurs include the Maldives and Sri Lanka, where there are massive tiger sharks. And these aren't Bahamas tiger sharks, these are sharks that have never seen a human being and are there to feed. There are bull sharks, silvertips, and dusky sharks, to name a few. On top of all of that, this little two-foot innocuous shark swims up rivers that are filled with mugger crocodiles, saltwater crocodiles, you name it. Don't get me wrong, the shark we're looking for is not Air Jaws. But the animals I'm going to have to avoid in order to find it are a hell of a lot scarier."

Joe's eyes had lit up. The game was afoot. Eric ran with the idea. And we left with a handshake deal to bring *Extinct or Alive* to Shark Week but also with the admonition that I couldn't produce the show on my own. We weren't proven, so we had to work with a team assigned to me by Discovery. I worried this was going to be Myanmar all over again, when I had an LA douchebag as my showrunner. But I managed to convince them to allow me to bring Mark. My team and I agreed that he was the most competent underwater shooter and the best scuba diver; and Jessica, my wife, also received a special (and ultimately fateful) dispensation to come along.

Things got off to a rocky start. Jess, Mark, and I were on a plane with this group of complete strangers, on the second or third leg of the flight to the Maldives, when somebody passed out in the aisle. Mark had been sitting near the guy and shouted for me to come to the back of the plane. He knew I was a trained medic and should be able to help. I got up, walked to the guy who was flat out on the floor, and started to assess what could be the problem. Suddenly, this fat, lumbering dude came running over, pushed me to the side, and shouted, "Stand down, I'm from New Jersey!"

In retrospect, this was hilarious. Being from New Jersey could have not been more irrelevant, and the guy passed out on the plane was simply very drunk. Medical assistance, whether from the Garden State or not, was not needed. Everyone calmed down once we got the drunk guy back in his seat. But the sizable gentleman who had taken charge was the assigned medic, and I had just gotten a taste of how this shoot was going to go.

We landed in the Maldives, most of us sober, and got to work. We went on several exploratory dives to get a feel for the conditions. We saw enormous tiger sharks, these bold, fierce giants, cruising on the currents, looking for food. We saw beautiful silvertips, compact and powerful at ten feet long. But we didn't see anything that resembled a Pondicherry shark. On land, we connected with impressive scientists in Sri Lanka, who had been fortunate enough to spot what they believed was a Pondicherry shark in Yala National Park about three years prior, which redirected our investigation to the river running through the park. A full upheaval of the plans and a quick flight across the Indian Ocean, and we were in a fishing port in Sri Lanka. Because we had a lot of ground to cover and wanted to increase our chances of success, Jess and I decided to divide and conquer. I was going to spend the next week sailing to the river mouth, exploring shallow waters along the way. Jess was going to follow some leads that we had on land. And most of the Discovery-assigned team, which had exhausted the planned budget for their shoot, headed home, leaving only a handful of us to continue the search.

Jess took off with one of the guys from Discovery, a man named Donald Schultz (you may recognize that name from his awesome Animal Planet show *Wild Recon*) from South Africa, who has since become a close part of our "shark crew." Together they were going to chase down reports about illegal pens where sharks were being kept for export on the aquarium trade. I, on the other hand, would spend the next week chumming thousands of pounds of fish all along the Sri Lankan coast, covered in rotting fish guts day in and day out, while doing everything I could to catch a glimpse of this slim and elusive animal. At the end of that week, though we'd run into several bull sharks and had spotted a blacktip, we had nothing on the Pondicherry. Jess and Donald had struck out at the first pen as well. It turned out to be full of juvenile blacktip reef sharks, which do look somewhat similar, but have subtle differences in size, shape, and markings. I was thinking that here I had proposed *Extinct or Alive* to Shark Week, searching not for Air Jaws but the gentlest of sharks, and was going to be hoisted by my own petard. Then I received a call from Jess.

"Hey, love. What's going on? Are you doing okay?"

It had been five days since we had spoken to each other, but she cut to the chase.

"Forrest, I think I've got a Pondicherry."

It turns out that Jessica, my beloved wife, who is a zoologist by trade but not someone specialized in tracking down wildlife, had gone into a fishing village with a picture of the Pondicherry on her iPhone. She was led to an old man sitting on two dead sharks that he had for sale. He had caught them in his gill net. Just like with my grandfather decades before, a sharp eye in a strange market had yielded exciting results. Jessica tried to barter with the man for the shark. But because she was this blonde, beautiful, American woman, he was set on selling her the more expensive lobsters he had for sale. He kept repeating the world "lobster," while she kept pointing at the shark. Eventually, he told her that the shark was worthless because it was so small, and he'd trade her for a pack of cigarettes. And so, for a pack of smokes, Jessica had acquired the fresh remains of an extinct species. Meanwhile, I was still multiple days out at sea, chumming in futility. We turned around as quickly as we could, connected with Jess in a fishing village in Yala National Park, and laid eyes on what is now one of the only archetype specimens of a Pondicherry in the world. Its stuffed remains are now on display in the Museum of Colombo in Sri Lanka.

And wouldn't you know it, the ratings rocked. Our show about a two-foot-long shark captured the highest ratings of the week outside of a celebrity special. People loved it because it was organic, an unscripted "docu-follow" where the outcome wasn't certain and the science wasn't bullshit. We brought viewers on one of our adventures and changed scientific history, not only finding a specimen of an extinct species but starting a conversation about expanding Yala National Park three miles into the ocean just to protect the Pondicherry.

The next year, I didn't have to go to Discovery; they came to me, which leads me to a point I want to make about the value of visible conservation. It is not about what I do. (Though, I have a blast doing it.) It is about what others are inspired to do. And my second stint with Shark Week was a perfect example.

Discovery wanted to up the ante from the Pondicherry. I didn't know how to do something crazier than find an extinct species. The network helpfully suggested that instead of one lost shark I find *three*. It would be great for ratings! I didn't know how this network note would play out in reality, but I signed up for the job. It was right about then that doubt entered my mind. There was a voice in my head shouting, "Forrest, you are never going to find those animals. You have agreed to do something no one could ever do. You are an idiot." So, I reached out for help and contacted a colleague of mine, Dr. Dave Ebert, a world-renowned shark scientist, a man who has named forty-plus species of shark. He's *the* guy, *the* elasmobranchologist, which is someone who studies cartilaginous fishes with five to seven vertical gill slits on each side. Sharks, baby! (And, sure, rays and skates, too . . .)

I told him what the network was expecting and asked him what he thought I should do.

"Why don't we team up and go to a region where there are multiple species of lost shark, and if we even get one of them, you know we'll be lucky."

It made sense both scientifically and entertainment-wise. We increased our chances by heading to a region where there were multiple missing animals. Discovery thought the idea was great, so *Extinct or Alive: Land of the Lost Sharks* kicked into gear. We were headed to a region in South Africa where three different species of shark had completely disappeared: the whitetip weasel shark, the ornate sleeper-ray, and the flapnose houndshark. I figured that finding even one would be a major victory. The chances of finding all three were astronomical. But we were going to do our best, and Discovery was more than glad to pay for us to try.

Another thing changed from the Pondicherry expedition: I got to bring my own team. I didn't have to work with disinterested cameramen who would otherwise be filming rap music videos (which describes one of the crew members from the previous year); I had the team I had so carefully assembled, who were ready to follow me anywhere, whose skills both as outdoorsmen and cameramen were unmatched, in my opinion, by anything any network could provide me with. So, the boys were back; and Mark, Mitch, Johnny, and I jumped on a plane to South Africa to meet up with Dave Ebert and the newest member of our shark team, Donald Schultz.

Even with spirits riding high, we had the same daunting task as ever before us: to somehow decode an unfamiliar ecosystem, to pry loose a reluctant animal from a vast and challenging landscape, and to do so in a matter of weeks. But this time we had set the bar insanely high. I'm not sure if it was arrogance or stupidity that made us think we could pull this off. There was no use wondering; we had a job to do.

In Kosi Bay, which is in the most remote part of South Africa, in the northeastern corner on the border with Mozambique, we began our expedition. We knew that maybe we would locate one of these animals, none of which had been seen in the previous thirty years and one of which hadn't been seen in the previous one hundred. To think that we'd find all three would be like calling your shot with a lottery ticket. Not helping matters was that I tore my groin on the third day. While we were launching our skiff from the beach, rocketing our bow over sets of waves on our way to open water, I slipped while trying to hold the boat steady in the surf. There was no mention of this in the show that aired, primarily because I didn't mention the injury to anyone. My leg was black from my knee to my groin. But, as ever, we had gone too far and there was too much riding on the outcome of the expedition, so I'd just have to grin and bear it. Later, I'd need to have surgery to break up the scar tissue around the tear.

Because Kosi Bay was so desperately remote, there were no harbors, marinas, or even stray docks from which to embark on our boats. Every day for a month, we'd have to fight through the breakers. And things weren't much easier once we reached our dive sites. The currents were violent. The extreme conditions led to some close calls. We screwed up our dive profiles, meaning we didn't keep correct track of our depths or paces of descent and ascent, and almost got mixed-air poisoning because of it. We lost Johnny for a time. Same with Mark. The strong currents and poor sight conditions made staying together almost impossible. But by using a BRUV, a baited remote underwater video system, an underwater trail camera essentially, we caught a quick glimpse of a shark with a unique profile. It was slim, had a protruding snout, and had a vigorous, flexible tail section. Our footage was quick and blurred, but it was distinct enough for Dr. Dave Ebert to declare it a sure sighting of one of our sharks, the whitetip weasel shark, only one specimen of which had ever been observed by science. It was the same kind of heart-palpitating evidence that I had discovered of the Zanzibar leopard, wherein a lost animal stalks into the frame for a moment and then back into the obscurity and safety of its environment. It only takes a few seconds to change the course of natural history.

Mission accomplished.

Well, partly.

STILL ALIVE

There were two more sharks on our list. We drove south from Kosi Bay to a town called Shelly Beach to begin our search for the ornate sleeper-ray. The nature of my arrival there goes to my point about the value of visible conservation. Apparently, I was a household name down in Shelly Beach—in a few households, anyway. Word had traveled that I was in South Africa looking for lost sharks. People knew the work I had been doing on *Extinct or Alive* and were eager to help. I received a phone call from a man named Adrian. Adrian, it turns out, was the cousin of a friend of the brother of the uncle of the sister of the nephew of our fixer. The connection was not a connection at all. But what Adrian had to tell us was worth listening to.

"Hi, Forrest. My name is Adrian, and I'm a dive master from Durban."

I thought that maybe he wanted to help us with scuba diving while we looked for sharks.

"Well," he continued, "I've been diving my whole life here. I've done thousands of dives and about six months ago, I captured film of something that I can't identify."

"Oh yeah, Adrian? How well do you know the species in the area?"

"Pretty well. I'm a dive master. I can go down and point out everything. But not six months ago. I saw this creature and don't know what it is. I can't find it on the Internet. I can't find it in books."

"Adrian, where are you?"

"I'm on the south end of town."

"Do you know where the Shelly Beach Ski Boat Club is?"

"Sure do."

"Can we meet there in thirty minutes?"

"You got it."

Adrian arrived at the club and sat down for a beer with Dave and me. He pulled out his iPad and starting swiping to the photos he had to show us. Dave lit up at the sight of the first one.

"Adrian, wow. That's Austin's guitar shark, a species that I named two years ago after my nephew Austin."

It was surreal for Dave to be surprised by footage of an animal he'd only seen as a dead specimen. Exciting though it was, it wasn't helping our cause. Then Adrian swiped to the next file.

"Hey, guys, what about this one?"

He flipped his iPad around, and wouldn't you believe it, Adrian, the local dive master, had high-definition video footage from his GoPro of the ornate sleeper-ray, the exact animal from our list. There it was: crystal-clear proof that this species was not lost to the world. In the short video, the thick-bodied and beautifully spotted ray was using its extendable jaws to search for prey in the sand, revealing a fascinating detail of its behavior. I will tell you now that of the discoveries we made on this expedition, this one mattered the most to me. My work had made such an impact in the world of wildlife caring and conservation that citizen scientists like Adrian had come out of the woodwork to find me, Forrest Galante, in this funky little town of Shelly Beach, South Africa, to say, "Look at this thing that I filmed that I can't identify." And that random thing that he had filmed and couldn't identify was the lost animal that we were looking for.

In this instance, I had inspired conservation. My message, the visibility of my work, had prompted an individual to get in touch, to join the cause, to save a species. This result showed me there would always be limits to what I could accomplish myself. But if I could move others to do the same work, then the impact on global wildlife could be limitless. Forrest Galante with one set of eyeballs looking for lost animals doesn't do a lot. But when the whole world, when millions of eyeballs go looking for things, anything can happen. I could have spent the next nine months on Shelly Beach. I could have spent the next nine years there and dove every day the way Adrian did, and I never would have found that ornate sleeper-ray. But guess what? Adrian happened to be the right person in the right place at the right time and shared his discovery with us right there at the Shelly Beach Ski-Boat Club.

By week four in the land of the lost sharks, we had found evidence of two of the three species of shark we had come to find. We had been extraordinarily fortunate. We had benefited from new technologies and from the proactivity of caring citizens. Some of that we could plan for, a lot of it we couldn't. And although we had already overachieved, there were still a few days left on our trip, and the flapnose houndshark remained unfound on our list. So, I called back to one of my first loves: casting a line into the water and hoping. Like the others, the flapnose had last been seen off the coast of South

Africa. But unlike the others, it had been lost to science for 120 years. This animal had been minding its own business even longer than the Fernandina Island tortoise had. Our strategy for finding it was simply to cast bait in the right place and wait. With squid on our hooks, we ran several lines from shore and hoped for the night to prove interesting. I stood there with my crew and Dave Ebert, with only the sound of the surf and the light of the stars to keep us company—well, along with the half-dozen crew members staring into brightly lit display screens of phones and cameras. Nearing midnight, line ticked from one of the reels, and the rod bent with the weight of life.

"Fish on," I shouted.

Dave jumped on the reel. I jumped into the surf and moments later had my hands around a two-and-a-half-foot-long shark with the same handsome head shape I had seen in drawings of the flapnose. I placed the shark in a plastic container filled with seawater and awaited confirmation of the find from Dave. (It really is convenient having the world's leading elasmobranchologist on hand.) Sure enough, on the underside of the fish, just above its mouth, were the telltale flaps that gave the shark its name. We had found all three species—all three sharks in thirty days. We had pulled just one fish from the surf that night, and it was the flapnose houndshark. This felt almost like an act of providence. And if Dave didn't know it before, he found out then, I was a hugger.

We splashed through the waves with joy for a few seconds and then calmed down enough to perform the necessary science, making sure we'd return the animal to the ocean as quickly as possible. We placed a tag through the shark's dorsal fin that would ride on the animal for three months and then float to the surface, relaying the tracked movements of the shark to a satellite.

I hadn't thought we could go bigger than the Pondicherry. But we had. We packed the discovery of three lost animals into one hour of television. There are no other shows that come even close to doing the same thing, that even dare to attempt it. Not only that, thanks to the talents and dedication of my crew, we produced an exceptional hour of television—far better than what I had managed when working with a cast of strangers on my first Shark Week. To date, and by far, it is my favorite episode I have ever made.

Forgive me if I sound proud. But what most excites me is that we have rewritten natural history eight times. The show had occasioned the rediscovery of eight lost species. The next highest number that a single human being has found of rediscovered species was one. I had found eight, smashing all preconceived notions of extinction.

TIRE CROC

TIRE CROC

My message was beginning to spread on its own. Not all extinct or lost animals were beyond saving. There was still hope for these animals and there were good reasons to invest in the health of their ecosystems. The message was inspiring involvement. In South Africa, Adrian had sought me out to help recover a lost species. Now, instead of my chasing leads, essentially waving my arms at scientists, asking, "Hey, I can find that thing you've lost! Let me be your mercenary," people are starting to approach me from all over the world, asking for my help with all sorts of problems. As you might expect, I get some pretty wild requests.

Not long ago, there was a tiger on the loose near Knoxville, Tennessee. And wouldn't you know it, but the Tennessee Wildlife Resource Agency got in touch, asking whether I had any info on tracking tigers in Eastern Woodlands. I told them that

I didn't think anyone did, but I bet that I could find their kitty. More frequently, I hear from people who want help tracking Bigfoot, or who believe they've encountered an extinct animal (the Mexican grizzly bear is a popular choice), or who just need help locating their pet cat. Aside from offering condolences about the cat, my answer is invariably no.

However, occasionally, something lands on your desk that demands your attention. A news story broke in Indonesia about a saltwater crocodile that had a car tire wrapped around its neck. They called it "the Michelin croc," or simply, "Tire Croc." My email started to flood with notes asking whether I could help this animal. The Indonesian government and its nature conservation agency BKSDA had released an international call for assistance.

This wasn't some "cryptofauna" lurking in the imagination of rural America. This wasn't someone's kitty stuck in a tree. This was a real animal with a real problem and a real solution. I investigated the history of who had attempted to capture the crocodile and what happened. I was beginning to think that we could do the job. Now, keep in mind, this was a saltwater crocodile in Indonesia, not a critically endangered animal. It wasn't rare or on the verge of extinction. Rather, this was an animal living in human waste in the city of Palu. It had been struggling with a tire around its neck for four years. Everybody and their grandmother had been trying to catch this thing to pull the tire off its neck, and the government had become so desperate that they were offering a reward to anybody who could come and save it. I contacted the BKSDA to introduce myself. I told them who I was and what I did, and I offered my help. They replied straightaway, "You found the Miller's grizzled langur! We'd love to have you. Please come and help us."

I went to Discovery Channel and said, "I don't care if this goes on TV or not. But how do you feel about doing some good in the world? Why don't we go save a crocodile? Why don't we make an impact here?"

Our great friend Joe Schneier told us to let him see what he could do. A funny thing happened in the week Joe took to confirm that Discovery would support the effort. A famous Australian crocodile trapper named Matt Wright hopped on a plane and went looking for Tire Croc. I alerted Discovery to the development. Maybe my services wouldn't be needed after all? Matt Wright was a serious tracker. He would probably catch the croc, and the problem would be solved. But after two weeks of trying, he headed home. So, Discovery told me to get on the next flight over. I've dealt with my fair share of crocodilians and have caught almost every kind, but if Matt Wright can't catch this animal, then something is up. There is some wacky business afoot.

I heard from Matt that Tire Croc was insanely shy and elusive. If you had spent the past four years of your life getting chased around by people with nets, spears, harpoons, snaggers, etc., you would probably be more than a little on edge. Crocodiles are already among the most instinctually intelligent creatures on Earth. They somehow seem to know whenever they've been targeted. It is one of the reasons why I love them so much. They're smart. They're ahead of the curve. The infamous man-eating crocodile Gustave in Burundi had been held responsible for the deaths of up to 300 people. A well-funded expedition was organized in the early 2000s to capture him, but once the hunters arrived, the crocodile, which people would otherwise see every day, seemed to disappear. They are so intuitive. They know when they've gone from hunter to hunted and they make themselves terribly scarce.

The saltwater crocodile in Indonesia's Palu River, already a highly adapted survivor, couldn't have been more wary. I knew we had a task ahead of us. Most crocodiles are caught with either nets or traps. I had nets and could fabricate a trap, but something told me that wouldn't be enough. What else could we do? A common and successful strategy, especially when catching alligators in the southeastern United States, is using a small harpoon. These harpoons are equipped with something called a "slip tip," which is a small, inch-long tip that pierces the animal just beneath the skin. Because crocodilians have such tough hides, once the harpoon punches beneath the skin, the barb of the harpoon can toggle subcutaneously, however the animal twists and turns, and will hold the creature on the line. And, for all its effectiveness, the harpoon leaves only an inch-long incision in the animal's skin and hopefully no deeper.

One thing that separates me from many biologists and wildlife scientists is that I repurpose a ton of weird tools. If you're like me and have tried throwing a harpoon with a string attached to the end of it, you won't have much luck hitting anything farther than ten feet away. I needed to find a way to bridge the theoretical effectiveness of the strategy with the difficulty of the conditions. Finally, I called up my buddy Lonnie Workman at PSE Archery.

"Lonnie, I got an idea. It's a little hairbrained, but I think you guys can do this."

I had his attention.

"What if we take your highest-powered crossbow, sighted to about twenty yards, and put a customized, fabricated crocodile tip on the end of the bolt? If I can get within thirty or forty feet of this croc, I shoot a bolt into the tail of the croc. The bolt would have a line attached to it, running to a float that I could work."

"No problem, man," Lonnie assured me. "People hunt crocs with crossbows all the time. How big is the thing you want to kill?"

"Here's the kicker: I don't want to kill anything. I have to do this safely and effectively, and we have to customize a tip and a bolt that can fly carrying high-powered line."

"Yeah, I think we can do that. We do have a lot of bow-fishing gear that could easily handle about a nine-foot gator. So, uh, how big is the animal?"

"It's about sixteen feet long and a thousand pounds."

"Oh, boy. Well, that's different."

The guys at PSE got to work creating an incredible crossbow, a real Forrest Galante custom job. Meanwhile, I prepared my snares, snags, hooks, tongs, and nooses—all the things that I use to catch crocodiles. I loaded up about twelve cases of gear, hopped onto a plane with Mitch and Mark, and headed to Indonesia. As you might expect, landing in a

Southeast Asian country with a high-powered crossbow is not so simple. I had a letter from the Indonesian president welcoming me to the country and thanking me for the effort I was taking on behalf of the animal, but it wasn't enough to persuade border patrol to let me into the country with my equipment. We spent half a day talking ourselves out of deeper trouble and made dozens of phone calls to the president's office. Eventually, we got the all clear and were able to head straight to downtown Palu, a city with more than 300,000 residents, where, oddly enough, this crocodile called home. We checked into a Best Western, which was a little bit different from my usual expedition base camp.

Understanding why this crocodile had been living with a tire stuck on its head wasn't hard to figure out. Driving around, we saw mountains of garbage everywhere. It was a sad sight. I told Mitch that we would need to feature this pollution whether we caught the croc or not. Even if we did, how much longer before we got another call about an animal that had eaten plastic bags or got two tires stuck around its neck or had a car battery dropped on its head? This one crocodile wasn't the problem. The problem was human waste and its mismanagement.

Back at the room, I started laying out all my tools for the job, a truly reliable kit now supplemented by my beautiful crossbow.

"Right, guys. Tonight's the night. Let's go find our croc."

Mitch and Mark were up and ready to go, but our fixer was surprised.

"Whoa, what do you mean?"

"We're gonna go catch the croc."

"We haven't met with BKSDA yet."

"Fine. Let's go meet with them."

"It's 6:30 p.m. They have gone home for the day. And you definitely can't catch the croc without their okay."

The usual frustration. You roll with it. As a scientist, I understand that. You don't just come into someone's home and help yourself to their fridge without saying hello first. We planned to head over to the organization's office first thing the next day. In the meantime, even though we were totally jet-lagged, we decided to hike along the banks of the river to see what we could see. The team grabbed the cameras. I grabbed the crossbow and threw it in the truck.

The river was only a two-minute drive from the hotel. This wasn't like putting fifty miles on a river in the Colombian Amazon. This was an utter mash-up of urbanity and raw nature. There were people everywhere. There were restaurants overlooking the water. This wasn't what I was used to when working on a wildlife expedition. Never in my life had I walked through piles of garbage along a riverbank where people were ordering dessert a few feet above my head. Not to mention, I was clad in camouflage and carrying a crossbow (not unlike when I used to tramp around Cayucos, California, hunting pigeons with a pellet gun). We were creating a massive spectacle.

The river was full of crocodiles. We were picking up eye-shine all over. But most of the animals were quite small. Then, in an eerie echo of my first night searching for the Rio Apaporis caiman, we spotted eyeshine belonging to a much larger individual. I had Mitch filming on my six using a night filter. I had my crossbow over my shoulder, loaded, because you never know. And there was Tire Croc, fully out of the water, lying on the riverbank, not twenty feet away from us. I backed up in silence. I put my left hand down to signal for Mitch to stop. This kind of communication had become second nature to us. We walked about 150 yards away from the croc. The first words that sprang to my mind were, "He was sitting *right there*."

We couldn't turn down the opportunity before us. Unlike the Rio Apaporis caiman that I spotted the previous year in the Amazon, which disappeared before we could get within thirty-five feet, this saltwater crocodile seemed perfectly content while we nearly stumbled upon it.

"Guys, this is it. We're gonna get that croc. We know where he is and the conditions are absolutely perfect. Let's do this."

Once again, our fixer saw things differently.

"You cannot."

I asked her why.

"This is Indonesia. If a white person comes here and does whatever he wants without permissions, they will make an example of you. You will go to jail."

This delay seemed utterly ridiculous to me. I had been asked to do a job and just wanted to be allowed to do it.

"Just trust me," our fixer said, "They are literally watching you right now. The secret police know you're here. Palu doesn't get tourists. That's how things work. Please wait."

I called the head of the BKSDA right then and managed to get through. I told him the crocodile was twenty feet away from me. Did I have permission to move on it? He responded with a hard no. Under no circumstances should I proceed with the capture. The croc was painfully close. We could be on a plane the next day with a job well done. But the risk of going to jail, which my crew and I had barely managed to avoid in Myanmar when filming *Face the Beast*, didn't seem worth chancing twice. We stood down. It was night number one. I thought if we found him in the first hour, we were going to find him again. Well, I was wrong about that.

The next morning, I visited the BKSDA office, but the head of the department was out for the day. Permission wouldn't be coming that day either. My frustration level was almost hard to control. Rather than go stir-crazy, sitting on my hands, I decided to make use of the time and found a local welder to fabricate an enormous crocodile trap. The cage was twenty-five feet long and eight feet wide, large enough for a sixteen-foot croc to waltz inside without feeling enclosed. While we waited for the trap to be built and for the head of the BKSDA to return, we ended up talking with some locals who told us that Tire Croc was actually someone's pet.

"What's that now?" I asked.

"Yes, a pet. The owner had used the tire and a rope to wrangle the crocodile. The crocodile wore the tire like a collar, and they'd pull him in with the rope and then let go."

I realized that if it were true that Tire Croc was someone's pet, then my job just got a lot easier. Crocodiles, as you see the world over, become conditioned to their keepers. We needed to find the guy who supposedly raised this animal. It was still day two of the ten we had allotted for the expedition, so we decided to investigate the lead. We learned that Tire Croc came from a former fish farm turned local tourist attraction, the main draw being a big pen full of crocodiles. I was told that the farm had been managed by a Korean man and his much younger Indonesian wife until the man abandoned his wife and farm ahead of an advancing cyclone. The cyclone absolutely flattened much of the city, the ex–fish farm included, leaving the young woman with a mostly destroyed tourist attraction to manage. The husband never returned, and the wife gave all the fish to her friends and let the crocs loose in the river.

We traveled to the site of the fish farm for a conversation with the former crocodile keeper, who had worked for the couple. His name was Palak Jamal. Speaking through a translator, he told us he believed that Tire Croc was named Acho. It was the biggest male crocodile that they used to have, and Mr. Jamal would be able to call him and the croc would come. I had just added to my croc-catching arsenal. We had a custom-made crossbow and a custom-made cage, and now we had the man who could literally call the croc toward us with the sound of his voice. Or so he said. I asked him whether he would accompany us to the river, and for $50 he happily agreed.

"Don't go up where you saw it by the bridge," he told us. "Go down to the river mouth. Because I know Acho. Acho likes the salt water."

Tire Croc

We went down to the river mouth and Mr. Jamal started shouting, "Acho, Acho, Acho," and slapping the water with a fish. He repeated the call a handful of times and a sizable crocodile popped up its head in the distance. Whether this was Acho or not, we couldn't tell. The animal was smart enough to expose only its snout and eyeballs above the surface of the water. Its neck, and whether there was a tire around it, remained out of view. That was all the action we'd get on day two. That night the skies tore open, dumping torrential rain and turning the rivers into churning mud.

This was a terrible turn of events. The rivers rose like crazy. Visibility was nothing, and the extra water in the system meant that animals had a far greater area to move around in. We stayed out all night in this deluge, hoping to record another sighting of the crocodile to pin its location for whenever we received permission to go forward with the capture. The next day we finally connected with BKSDA. I am not blaming the agency for the delay at all. This is what bureaucracy looks like. This was Indonesia, a very strictly governed place, and if you were to make a wrong move—say, by allowing an American television personality to harpoon a giant croc in the middle of a city without even having met with him first—you would be out of a job. My conversation with the head of the BKSDA was tremendous. He was fully briefed on who I was and what I was trying to do and simply wanted to provide the support I needed to succeed. We were ready to go, but I had to ask him.

"What would have happened if I'd gone and tried to catch the croc two days ago?"

"Oh, good thing you didn't do that without us. You would have been in big trouble."

Now, when the head of an Indonesian government organization says, "big trouble," you know he means it. I realized I had made the right decision. If I hadn't, I wouldn't be recounting this story in the pages of a book, I'd be sitting in jail in Indonesia.

He told me they had been trying to capture Tire Croc for years and everyone had failed: the BKSDA itself, of course, but also crocodile experts from France, Italy, and, most recently, Australia. With the go-ahead finally secured, we combed the river up and down for a full day, returning at about 1:30 a.m. to the bridge where we had spotted the croc sitting on the bank when we first arrived. There I swept the beam of my flashlight over the water and picked up the telltale eyeshine of a giant crocodile—and, sure enough, it was Tire Croc. Unfortunately, he wasn't providing us with the same kind of shot we had the first night, when he had allowed us to approach to within forty feet. This time he had situated himself in the rapids of the swollen and raging river, which had risen nearly a dozen feet because of the rain. But at least he was there.

Still, a specially built croc-crossbow does give you a little bit of confidence. I had taken more than 150 practice shots at home and knew I was accurate with the scope to about ten yards. Accuracy was important in order not to harm the animal. So long as I stuck my harpoon in the fatty deposits at the base of the tail, it would cause only minimal and superficial damage. Our setup was to shoot the dart into the tail; the dart would run on a tether to a float, and the float would allow us to track the crocodile. Once we located the float, we could put a net around the area and pull the croc in. Easy, right? Of course, there was nothing easy about it. We were talking about a sixteen-foot animal that had reportedly killed at least three people. By necessity, we were planning to create a very dangerous situation. Not only that, but I was responsible for the use of a high-powered crossbow. If I took a bad shot near the animal's spine or organs, I was likely going to kill the crocodile—and that was a risk that I wasn't willing to take.

The croc had by now figured out that someone was looking for him. The four years of persecution, well-intentioned though it was, had made this animal extraordinarily cautious. Even though it was the apex predator and would kill you in a heartbeat, it knew when to keep far away. I put on my red light, which is a spectrum of light that crocodiles cannot see, grabbed my crossbow, and told Mitch, "Grab my six," meaning to film me from behind. As we headed over, I saw the animal's nose, head, and first third of its body resting out of the water; and I could see the tire. This was a huge animal. Its head was three and a half feet long. His head alone stood taller than half of my body. And there he was in all his glory, facing upstream in the rapids, about fifteen or twenty yards out. I pulled up the crossbow. It was loaded with bolts in place and tips ready to toggle. I looked through the sight and lined up the croc in the crosshairs. And I waited. And I waited some more. I wasn't seeing a clear shot. As I wrote above, I would much rather leave Indonesia empty-handed than with knowing that I had injured this animal or worse. After about fifteen minutes of staring through the crosshairs, with my arms beginning to quiver and shake, I whispered to Mitch.

"Hand me the noose."

I was going to try to do this the old-fashioned way. Even though he was sunk within the rapids, Tire Croc was close enough to the riverbank that I could potentially wrangle him to shore with my extending noose, the same one I used to catch the Rio Apaporis caiman. So, I put down the crossbow, lifted the noose, and began to reach over—and the river exploded. Sixteen feet of reptilian muscle erupted in the water, spraying us all as the animal bolted, not to be seen again that night.

Even after the near miss, even after the delay, the rain, and the squandering of a perfect opportunity on day one, it was only day three of a planned ten-day expedition, and I would gladly extend my time if need be. We had already seen the croc two or three times, so I figured we'd have a few more shots and that we would succeed.

The next morning at 9:30 a.m., downstairs at the Best Western breakfast buffet, where we were stuffing ourselves with *nasi goreng* (Indonesian fried rice), our translator, Dian, came through the door and sort of slumped into a chair at the table. He had a very heavy look in his eyes.

"What's wrong, Dian?"

"I've got very bad news, Forrest."

"Well, what's that?"

He took out a folder and slid it across the table in front of me. In the folder was a letter from the president himself writing, "Effective immediately, BKSDA is to close as a government organization, and you are no longer able to conduct your targeting of the tire croc, for risk of exposure to COVID-19."

We had left the United States on March 5, 2020, when there was only whispering that the novel coronavirus was spreading beyond Wuhan, China. We had worn masks on our flight, but no one had seemed overly concerned. In the four days since, the pandemic had spiked, and governments were locking down. I wish I could say I grasped the magnitude of what was happening right away. But, like so many others, I did not. My initial response was that this was an overreaction like what had happened in response to swine flu and bird flu. I told Dian to get BKSDA on the phone. I asked them whether they were ready to catch a croc today.

"Oh, no, no, no, no," was the response, "Have you not seen the news from the president?"

The virus was very real, and panic was sweeping across Indonesia. Still, I maintained a hopeful perspective. After hanging up with BKSDA, I turned to Mark and Mitch.

"Why don't we wait it out two weeks, guys? We're in a very comfortable Best Western, and I know Palu is not the most exciting city in the world, but I'm guessing in a week to ten days this whole thing will blow over, the same way SARS and all the rest did, and then we can get back to work."

But after a little bit of discussion, the guys decided to head home immediately. They were worried about their families and didn't want to risk whatever was going to happen in Indonesia.

"Go for it," I told them, "Don't worry about it. I'm here. I've got my two local crew members working with me. Just leave me a camera, and we'll get this croc job done."

They took me at my word and left on a plane that night. But the writing was on the wall, written large enough for even me to see it. By the next morning, outgoing flights were shutting down and BKSDA had been completely abandoned. If I didn't get on a flight that day, who knew how long it would be before I could come home.

I made it out by a day. If I had resisted any longer, I would be living in Palu now and probably cleaning rooms at the Best Western. I came directly home, or tried to. First, I had to sit in quarantine for ten days, where I kept thinking that I'd head back to Indonesia in two or three weeks, whenever the lockdown would lift. But, as we'd find out, the lockdown would remain in place until at least January 1, 2021. There was no rushing back to Indonesia. Tire Croc would remain Tire Croc for a little while longer. Thankfully, a crocodile can go a full year without eating, and Tire Croc was still eating. He wasn't suffocating yet and maybe had another three or four years of life with the tire still in place. Even if I couldn't return this year or the next, there would still be an opportunity to help this animal.

Though I was bummed to return home prematurely without having completed the job, we still made a good hour of television, one that highlighted the problems of pollution and animal mistreatment. Discovery aired the program on Earth Day, and it topped ratings for the day.

Along with everyone else, I was faced with the inconvenience, fear, and uncertainty brought on by the COVID-19 pandemic. We couldn't travel. We couldn't even plan to travel by sending scouts ahead of our expeditions. I had been filming television for the previous three years almost without a break. *Extinct or Alive* had turned into an all-encompassing job. But now there was no way to do it. Although this was frustrating, my work on television had always been a means to an end, the end being conservation awareness that results in the protection of ecosystems and species. So, with normality on pause, I'd have to figure out another means.

I didn't have to look far or think hard to see that the coronavirus itself was signaling an alarm about the health of our planet. With millions infected and hundreds of thousands dead, with every aspect of our daily lives altered, we seemed to have forgotten that the only reason we were in such a painful situation was because of our own mistreatment of our fellow creatures, of animals themselves—because this terrible virus entered the human microbiome from the stalls of a wet market in Wuhan, China.

EPILOGUE

EPILOGUE

Flying home from Indonesia, I realized the pandemic was presenting an important opportunity to continue my mission in a new way. In my search for lost animals, I found myself time and again in local markets, much like my grandfather, looking for unusual animals on sale and talking to hunters about what lived in their forests, lakes, and rivers. Even though I would be focused on the task at hand, it was impossible to ignore the kinds of places these were. These weren't your Sunday farmers markets in the town square; these were wet markets, where wild animals were kept alive, caged or tied to a post, until a customer would order part or all of the animal and then watch as the vendor butchered the animal right then and there. These are not pleasant places to spend one's time. Not only are they heartbreaking and cruel, but they pose a staggering threat to humanity. They are petri dishes for zoonotic diseases to leap from wildlife to human beings. Having discovered, along with the rest of the world, that it was in just such a wet market in Wuhan, China, where someone consumed an infected bat and started the COVID-19 pandemic, I had my latest subject, one that would allow me to deliver a message to viewers about what we owe to our natural inheritance, and that will lead to a final message I want to share in this book.

In the strange months that followed my return to California from Indonesia, I pulled together a presentation on the threat posed by wet markets. I combined footage I had shot on my iPhone, long before I started making television, with all the relevant footage from my time working with Animal Planet. I contacted experts from around the world, including those from the Wildlife Conservation Society, to ask them how zoonotic diseases worked and whether our current pandemic was an outlier or a sign of what was to come. To a scientist, everyone told me that the coronavirus had been a ticking time bomb. The scientific community had known it was coming. I'm not writing this with 20/20 hindsight. These scientists—Dr. Christian Walzer and Dr. Cortni Borgerson, for example—had been publishing papers and delivering talks for years, presenting the evidence of our vulnerability. They had warned that if our behavior did not change, then we could expect to face a highly contagious zoonotic disease to which humans had little or no immunity and that could potentially kill millions of people. If these were the predictions, and if these predictions had come true, then why weren't we making a bigger deal about the source of the contagion? Why weren't we shouting to shut down wet markets, fighting for regulations that would protect all of us? I don't have the answer to that. But I do have the ability to make some noise in the hope that I'll inspire others to care. And so, when Eric and I discussed the best way of airing this new exposé, we agreed that Animal Planet wouldn't be the right place. News doesn't live on Animal Planet. What we had to say was going to be news to a lot of people. We needed to find a partner who understood the urgency and could help us reach an engaged, issue-driven viewership.

VICE News has been the home of edgy journalism on HBO for the past several years. It is a very different place than the earthy confines of Animal Planet, but it was perfectly suited to the difficult stories and images I had to share. When we took a meeting with them, I explained (over Zoom) that we were all locked in quarantine because of a wet market and the reason their office was closed was because of a wet market. In response, one of the producers bravely raised her hand to ask, "Well, what's a wet market?"

They had all been confined to their homes for five months by that point and yet didn't know why. (For the record, a wet market provides fresh meat to communities that do not have refrigeration.) At first my head was spinning because of her revelation, but it only took me a moment to realize, and then to convince them, that her answer was precisely why my show needed to be made. They asked straightaway how many episodes I could complete. I wanted to make twenty, of course, but suggested that we create four one-hour segments that visited wet markets in different parts of the world—in Africa, Europe, Asia, and South America—to cover the various styles. So, even with *Extinct or Alive* sidelined by COVID-19, we were finding a way to continue making a difference and hopefully making change.

And change is imperative.

I came to see the pandemic as a chance for all of us to understand that if we can treat animals and the ecosystem with a little bit of respect, then we can save ourselves. If I saved an elephant in Africa, for example, a plumber in Chicago isn't going to care all that much. He's not planning a trip to Africa. He's never going to see that animal. So, it may be difficult for him to understand why saving that animal matters. However, if I told that plumber that if I don't save that elephant in Africa, then that plumber will be stuck in his small apartment for the next year, wearing a mask every time he answers the door and waiting for a vaccine to be developed to immunize him from an animal-borne contagion, maybe he'd care a bit more. Actually, I bet he'd care a lot. That's the point COVID demands that I make. The whole planet is connected. Every single living thing is connected.

Our world is like a giant game of Jenga. When you pull out one block at the beginning of the game, nothing much happens. You still have a very stable tower. Then you laugh and say, "Your turn." The next person pulls out another block. Still nothing. The tower remains very stable. Now, fast-forward ten moves and the tower has gone wobbly. Fast-forward another ten and you're doing everything within your power, conceptually and physically, to slide out another piece and keep the tower from collapsing on the table. We have reached a point in humanity's relationship with the earth's natural systems that if we move another three or four proverbial Jenga blocks—for example, if we don't commit to clean energy, control plastics, build smarter cities, and preserve our wildernesses—then there is going to be a global-scale collapse. But you, by respecting and educating yourself and caring, can make change on a global scale to slow down this process, and maybe, just maybe, we can start putting a couple of blocks back into the Jenga tower. And maybe the great interconnected balance of our world won't seem so shaky.

I truly hope that by the time you read this the pandemic will be a thing of the past. I hope we'll have found a vaccine. I hope the vaccine works. I hope we've produced it on a mass scale, immunizing not just the rich but the needy, and I hope we've learned a lesson. It's actually a wonderful thing to envision that future, because the lesson of the present is tough, even if it is necessary.

As you might expect, the logistics of filming an internationally set exposé during a pandemic were pretty challenging. But thanks to all the cherished connections I had made around the world, the show featured in-country hosts in each location—an Indonesian woman, a Peruvian woman, an African doctor of pangolins, and an Albanian farmer—who investigated the abhorrent practices taking place in their local markets. And though I do want to strike a hopeful note in saying that the coronavirus afforded us an opportunity to learn from our mistakes, it also highlighted the absolute necessity of learning that lesson. Because if we don't learn it, the next pandemic is going to be worse.

Though the point of a wet market is to provide fresh meat in places where there isn't refrigeration, which is most of the world, the meat is rarely that fresh. If someone decides they want to take a baboon arm home for dinner, the rest of the animal lies in the market stall, steaming in the tropical sun until the next customer springs for the other arm. There you have an immunocompromised animal that's been left in unsanitary conditions. But, obviously, you could buy more than just a baboon at the market. That carcass may have contacted a bat, a pangolin, or a dog—animals that would never meet in the wild and that would never be so stressed and immunocompromised. If a virus from a pangolin jumps to a bat and then to a dog, something that would never happen in nature, that virus will undergo an unprecedented mutation. (Viruses are always mutating as they evolve around animal immune systems. It is why the common cold keeps coming back around year after year. You might have had a cold last year, but, sorry, you're not immune, because you're getting the new version this year.) And when a virus, formed within the ungodly muck of a wet market, jumps to a dog, the viral mutation that occurs within the dog makes humans uncommonly susceptible to catching it. So, the individual who consumes a dog not only commits a shameful act, but he becomes patient zero.

The Spanish flu of 1918 and 1919, which killed tens of millions of people worldwide, had a comparable animal origin, springing from North American birds. Avoiding the next Spanish flu, a viral pandemic even deadlier than COVID-19, will depend on our capacity and willingness for change. Though I know that forceful and dynamic TV programming can inspire others to care about wildlife, the scale of change needs to be even greater. To secure the future, we must make change on a legal and constitutional level. The point of the investigation into international wet markets was to persuade leaders in the featured countries to take some kind of action, whether that is to ban them outright, regulate them, or provide refrigeration. And I can tell you that achieving legal change requires even more toughness and perseverance than it does to search for extinct animals. (After all, the lost animal doesn't have its own lawyers.)

In 2018, on Capitol Hill in Washington, DC, I testified on nonlethal mitigation of human-predator conflict, speaking about how to make actual change. In layman's terms, when an animal and a person are having a problem, how do we fix that problem without shooting the animal in the head and declaring the problem solved? It has been humanity's go-to strategy for eons (plus or minus the guns). When a tiger attacked a village, they would call the "Great Hunter" to kill the tiger and eliminate the conflict. Well, now we don't have many tigers left in the wild, right? Fewer than 4,000, according to the World Wildlife Foundation. So, we can't just shoot the tiger every time a tiger threatens livestock in a village or even attacks someone. Before long, we'd have no more tigers and the same number of people and livestock.

I arrived in Washington, DC, straight from the bush. I got off the airplane, drove to the hotel, trimmed my beard, and donned a suit for the first time in probably three years. Within a few hours of my arrival, I was seated before the Senate Committee on Environmental and Public Works, chaired by Senator John Barrasso of Wyoming. I felt like I was swimming in a different kind of ocean surrounding by a new breed of sharks that sensed my vulnerability. I was speaking alongside two other wildlife experts—one who worked with bears in Montana and another from California who worked with sharks—and we essentially pressed the case that change needed to happen now for the sake of predators and the eco-systems of which they were a vital part. After we completed our presentations, the senators turned the tables on us, ac-knowledging that change sounded well and good, but *how* were we going to create this change? The senator from Mon-tana asked directly what he should do if a bear were attacking citizens in Montana.

"Tell me how to solve the problem."

I jumped at the chance to answer. As you know, I have a fascination for repurposing technologies and tools—whether they come from fishing, hunting, or the military—for applica-tion in wildlife sciences. And I have seen time and again how a hybrid approach is often a successful approach. I answered the senator by telling him that an increase in funding to universities for technological research could provide a solution in the near term. For example, the problem of a grizzly bear entering a schoolyard isn't so different from the problem of a leopard killing livestock in an African village. You could put up a fence, certainly. But how much fence is enough or too much? It would look pretty silly to have fencing wherever there is the *possibility* of a wildlife encounter. So, in the case of the leopard, instead of shooting the animal once it enters the village, why not find a way to deter it? Why not create animatronic decoys, as I suggested to the senator, that are motion activated and programmed to recognize a leopard with artificial intelligence technology on its trail camera? Once the device identifies a leopard, it projects the sound of the leopard's natural enemy, the lion, out into the bush. The leopard is going to hightail it out of there. My suggestion may have sounded a little dreamy and ambitious, but the technology already existed! By funding the right scientists who understood grizzly bear behavior, a decoy could be created that would prove just as repellant to the bear as the sound of the lion did to the leopard.

We did not have to reinvent the wheel. All we had to do was give universities, scholars, and engineers a bit of freedom to explore the applications of technology within the context of wildlife science, molding them to the purpose of understanding and conserving species. The results wouldn't be perfect the first time out, but you would eventually have successful conflict mitigation, effectively saving the person, the livestock, and the predator, all while preserving the integrity of the ecosystem. After testifying, shaking a lot of hands, and looking like a real jackass, if you asked me, in my buttoned-down suit, the committee released a million dollars in the form of Theodore Roosevelt Memorial Grants, administered by the American Museum of Natural History. Funneling money to researchers throughout North America and charging them to generate new solutions to age-old problems was a thrilling outcome. I was gratified not just for turning the wheel of government but for the commitment to the future. Here we were believing in all of the solutions that were yet to come.

It was a special moment when my public advocacy intersected with policy making. I shook my head to think that if I hadn't ventured to share my stories way back when *Naked and Afraid* shined a little light on me (all of me), there was no way I'd be giving my opinion to the decision makers of the world. You just never know when your opportunities are going to come along, and you never know how far passion and belief will carry you. But though I have carried my passion for wildlife a long way, I know it isn't nearly enough.

I see the species we have saved as a Band-Aid on a much larger wound. What I have done on *Extinct or Alive* is of course well-intentioned but limited in its effect. Even the new solutions that address human-predator conflict will be regional at best. The problem we face is global. The problem we face is inside every human heart and mind. The whole world needs to change its ideas about living in harmony with nature, respecting wildlife, and protecting the places where wildlife lives. I can't think of a better way to put it, but we need to realize that sustainability is cool. As Sir David Attenborough would tell you, humanity must shift its focus from growth to balance. And balance can be achieved only through awareness and wise management of our natural inheritance.

For a long time, maybe forever, there has been a virulent strain of masculinity, which I believe is called "toxic masculinity" these days, that celebrates man over nature, that really digs it when some guy clad in camo, sitting in a tree, rifles down a deer from 200 yards away. He'd hoof it over to his kill, take a few bloodstained photos, and consider himself a man until the next hunting season. But for the year in between, he wouldn't see the deer overwinter, he wouldn't see the fawns born, and he wouldn't see the animals move about a changing landscape as spring awakened. He wouldn't be in touch. He'd be a taker, someone who pulled from a resource only to assure himself of his dominance, without understanding the energy, time, and intricacy required to provide him with a fresh kill. I don't mean to malign every hunter. I myself hunt, albeit with fins and a spear gun. Steve Rinella of the show and website *MeatEater* is a great example of someone who understands the preciousness of the resource he enjoys. But widespread in the culture, I have seen a callousness, a thoughtlessness that doesn't bode well for the conservation of wild spaces.

I'm not saying that once you finish reading this book, you need to devote your entire life to conservation and animal rights activism. But if you would understand and help others understand that it is a whole lot harder to walk up to a deer quietly, sit down, and take a beautiful photograph of it with a camera than it is to kill it from a quarter of a mile away, then that would continue a necessary shift in perception. We need to change our consumptive and destructive mindset. And if every person in the world doesn't think that chest-thumping, nature-conquering dude is cool anymore, but instead thinks that living in harmony with nature and appreciating it, respecting it, and valuing it is beautiful and essential to our very existence, then I think massive change is possible.

What I will venture at the end of this book is to tell you to get outside. And if you already go outside a lot, go outside more. Find places you haven't been. Notice animals you haven't seen. Experience an ecosystem. Become more conscious about how you connect with the wild world. The hunter who drives two hours every fall to harvest a deer isn't going to miss that deer once it is removed from the forest. He is not connected to where that animal lives. But the more you connect with wild systems, the more you respect them; and the more you respect them, the more you care. It is a cycle of stewardship that begins when you spend time outdoors. The forests, jungles, mountains, and seas will rush into you, will transform you, if you let them.

As a scientist, I can't tell you that the earth cares about you, but it without a doubt sustains you; and if you care for the earth, you will be repaid tenfold. Whether you spend your time in Borneo chasing extinct monkeys, in Colombia dodging drug cartels for caiman, or in Central Park watching for migratory birds, it doesn't matter. Let it inspire you to make big choices, as it did with me, like starting a career in wild-life, science, or conservation. Let it inspire you to make small choices, often the hardest ones, like forgoing the coffee cup, the plastic bag, or the hamburger. Find a way to make your small choices add up.

TAKING ACTION

If you are ready to make change in the world, rather than just reading about it, any of the organizations listed below will guide you on where and how you can make a difference. Tell them Forrest sent you!

Wildlife Conservation

Association of Zoos and Aquariums

Defenders of Wildlife

US Fish and Wildlife Service

Wildlife Conservation Society

World Wildlife Fund

Aquatic

American Rivers

Monterey Bay Aquarium

Oceana

Ocean Conservancy

Project AWARE

Ecosystems

Conservation International

The Nature Conservancy

Rainforest Alliance

The Sierra Club

World Land Trust

Trusted Species-Based Organizations

Jane Goodall Institute

The National Audubon Society

Panthera

Saola Working Group

Turtle Conservancy

Zambezi Elephant Fund

ACKNOWLEDGMENTS

I dedicated this book to my mother because she always supported and believed in me. As a kid, whenever I wanted to find a cool fish or keep a snake in the house, she never said no. Instead, she would help me learn where to find it, how to catch it, and where to go, and then would take me there. She fueled my passion and desire, and I am forever grateful.

My wife, Jessica, whom I've known since I was fifteen years old, is my rock. She believed in me back when I was making $14 an hour as a biology field tech. She believed in me when I decided to leave academia to pursue media. We lived on her part-time teacher's salary for years. She never complained, never grumbled, and always believed that I would make it. And if it weren't for Jess's grounding over the years, I would have gone very far off the rails.

My family, in general, have been so wonderful and supportive, and they are all important to me. My stepdad, Chris, and my sister, Summer (whom I relentlessly tortured when we were kids), have had to put up with a lot. My grandad, who has passed on now, was an inspiration. My grandmother is so full of love and so proud, which means the world to me. I am grateful to my cousins in the United Kingdom, who were there for us when we got kicked out of Zimbabwe; my aunt, who helped us when we came to California; and my niece, who is pursuing her own path in the protection of our environment.

I want to extend thanks to my friends from college—Ricardo, Jordan, Adam, and even Nick—who are still to this day my best friends. It doesn't matter where life takes us; we always find a way to make wonderful memories on adventures every year.

Huge thanks to Patrick DeLuca and Eric Evangelista. Without them, I would be nowhere. Without Eric taking a chance on me and Patrick wanting to work with me, I don't know where I'd be. Probably still a field tech running around tagging rattlesnakes.

I'd like to give thanks to Joe Schneier, Howard Swartz, Erin Wanner, Keith Hoffman, Sarah Russell, Scott Lewers, Amy Introcaso-Davis, and the rest of the Animal Planet and Discovery Channel teams, who are always supportive and willing to take chances on me. They're more like friends than colleagues. Again, I don't know where I'd be without them.

Acknowledgments

There is also a world of collaborators who have made my work possible, including Cortni Borgerson, Dave Ebert, and James Leu, to name a few. Institutions such as Goliath Safaris, my family's safari business; UC Santa Barbara, especially the College of Creative Studies, which allowed me to go to college as a bit of a misfit; Native Range, the first biological company to hire me; World Wildlife Foundation; the BKSDA; Jungle Run, the Indonesian fixers who are always so helpful; SAIAB, the South African Institute for Aquatic Biodiversity; the Turtle Conservancy. All of these and many, *many* others that, unfortunately, I do not have space to name, are wonderful scientific institutions that have helped me advance my love and passion by letting me collaborate with them. If it weren't for those fellow scientists and institutions, none of this would be possible.

In terms of writing this book, I could not have done it without the help of my amazing attorney/friend Todd Shill; my literary agent, Brandi Bowles, and her team at United Talent Agency; and my excellent editor, Dan Ambrosio, and his team at Hachette Books. And I wish to thank Michael Signorelli for his unending patience in helping me tell this story.

The people who help me behind the scenes keep this ship sailing. I am so grateful for all the help of my post and planning team, including Hayley Martin, who spends countless hours on research; Ethan Friedman for getting the word out about our work; Steven Rockmael, without whom I would likely still be stuck in the jungles of Indonesia; Josh Kleefeld for all the sleepless nights of downloading and delivering footage; Christopher Stout, who takes our crazy journeys and makes them into compelling stories; and the rest of the post team.

And then there is my field crew: first and foremost, Mitchell Long. He's been with me since the very beginning of *Extinct or Alive*. He's literally my right-hand man. I can't even fathom the idea of doing a show without him. He's the first person I turn to. He strives for perfection. He puts up with me when I scream at him and when I drag him through the mud and make him face deadly crocodiles. And he does it all with a smile on his face and an incredible attitude.

Johnny Harrington started working with me at the age of twenty-three for a free wet suit. Now he's incredibly successful and arguably one of the best underwater cameramen in the world. He is one of my best friends in the whole world and a most valued member of my team.

Mark Romanov, Trevor "The sound-o" Robertson, James Brantley, Jesse Colaizzi, and Josh Amero are super valuable members of my team and go-to's no matter the situation—no matter how hard it gets, where we're traveling, or how terrible it's going to be, these are guys who will drop everything to help me out and make an adventure into great television. And without those guys, that production team, I don't think we would be nearly as successful as we are. They are the hardest group of badasses I've ever met. And they are wonderful to work with.

Thank you, everyone. You mean the world to me.